A Birch Lane Press book

Published by Carol Publishing Group

Birch Lane Press is a registered trademark of
      Carol Communications, Inc.

Editorial Offices: 600 Madison Avenue, New York, N.Y. 10022

Sales and Distribution Offices: 120 Enterprise Avenue,
      Secaucus, N.J. 07094

In Canada: Canadian Manda Group, P.O. Box 920, Station U,
      Toronto, Ontario M8Z 5P9

Queries regarding rights and permissions should be addressed to
      Carol Publishing Group, 600 Madison Avenue, New York, N.Y. 10022

Carol Publishing Group books are available at special discounts for bulk purchases, for sales promotions, fund raising, or educational purposes. Special editions can be created to specifications. For details, contact Special Sales Department, Carol Publishing Group, 120 Enterprise Avenue, Secaucus, N.J. 07094

Design: Morris Taub    Production: Wendy Crumpler, Sue Walsh

Photographs with permission of The New York Daily News, Associated Press and United Press International. Hirschfeld drawing on page 117 © Al Hirschfeld. Reproduced by special arrangement with Hirschfeld's exclusive representative, the Margo Feiden Galleries, New York.

Manufactured in the United States of America

10 9 8 7 6 5 4 3 2 1

Library of Congress Cataloging-in-Publication Data

Plaskin, Glenn.
      Turning point: pivotal moments in the lives of America's celebrities /
by Glenn Plaskin.
      p.  cm.
      "A Birch Lane Press book."
      ISBN 1-55972-138-3
      1. Celebrities—United States—Biography. 2. United States—
Biography.  I. Title.
CT220.P57  1992
920.073—dc20                                  92-26134
                                                      CIP

To my baby, Katie,

the sweetest turning point I've known—

a daily reminder

of innocence, loyalty, and love

# CONTENTS

# P R E F A C E

Sweet-smelling and innocent, trusting and unashamed, the newborn baby sleeps away the days safe from worry, longing, and fear. Safe from problems. Safe from a dangerous place. Safe not for long.

Lucky kids have parents who know how to love them without smothering them, who know how to discipline them without abusing them. Lucky kids grow up with a positive self-image.

More typically, terrible things happen. The unsuspecting child—hungry only for love and acceptance—instead encounters multifaceted abuse: emotional abandonment, neglect, violence, manipulation, and unhealthy control. Subtle or blaring, these traumatic experiences oppress the vulnerable child.

Later, in "adulthood," the challenges of making money and love are oftentimes overwhelming. Then, add to all of this pivotal, unexpected moments that appear from nowhere.

You may call such events fate or destiny, or luck, or accident, or self-fulfilling prophecy resulting from a chain of past events. I call them turning points, key moments that change everything.

First comes the *crisis*—the physical disease, the car accident, the love affair, the ailing baby, the addiction, the divorce, the financial triumph, the whatever. The tears. The manic high—or low. The bad dream—and daydreams. Your world is helplessly thrown into the air, your safe kingdom invaded for better or worse. What to do and how to do it?

Next comes the *battle*—the fight up from the problem requiring *change*. Refreshing, agoniz-ing, and terrifying—change can make us quiver in discomfort. But a turning point, unrelenting once it begins, forces such change upon us. Everything we viewed as settled and safe is open to *reassessment*.

And the result of the turn can be a *new way of living*, a *renewed sense of self-love*. The lost and discouraged little kid in each one of us has had the chance to peel back protective layers and emerge with a new, stronger skin.

Battles waged and lessons learned comprise the heart and soul of this book—accidentally born in the back of my New York City taxicab in July 1989. That day, as a daydreaming reporter for the *New York Daily News* increasingly struck by the meaninglessness of asking movie stars about their latest films, I pulled from my wallet a business card.

For some reason, I began to think about Dear Abby and Ann Landers, and my own therapy, and wrote down "Turning Point" on the card. How about a service-oriented column, a succinct vignette that allowed people to talk about their own fates and crises? I liked it right away, and I hope you do too.

The columns collected here were originally printed alongside Ann Landers and Joyce Brothers in the *New York Daily News*, as they continue to be. Without the luxury afforded by the full-length profile, I tried very hard to pack into ten column inches the beginning, middle, and end of stories I found compelling.

Throughout, I'm more interested in the inside than the outside of people. Makes me feel warmer, safer, just like at first. Tell me about your *mother*, not your movie. Tell me about how you came from nowhere to somewhere, not about your new diet. How did you reformulate the recipe of your life? How did you come closer to happiness?

What kept you going when nothing went right?

Most memorable: An outraged Elizabeth Taylor hollering across the room, incensed by AIDS and the cruelty of homophobia, then beginning to cry as she remembered Rock Hudson's death; an unmade-up Joan Rivers, subdued and painfully thin, recounting slamming her hand across the medicine cabinet and sweeping to the floor the medications of her husband, Edgar Rosenberg, who had committed suicide; a fragile Joan Kennedy just out from a Dominican monastery, feeling refreshed and hopeful that she could beat, yet again, an uphill fight with alcoholism; the snake-entwined LaToya Jackson, petrified and shaking, convinced her own family would attempt to kidnap her to prevent the publication of her autobiography; a radiant Carol Burnett throwing in a load of laundry during our interview, relating her twenty-year ascent to self-esteem; and Julio Iglesias and Victoria Principal, both transformed after near-fatal car accidents.

But most poignant: First, not long before his death, Michael Landon recounted being "raped" as a college student, having his long hair chopped off and testicles covered with Atomic Balm. Battered as a child, he said, and shattered as a young adult, Landon left college penniless and depressed, searching for a new life. His final words centered on the love for his many children and nurturing along their self-esteem.

Then the splendiferous Patti LaBelle, haunted by the spirits of her three sisters, all of whom died of cancer. Now frightened for her own life, filled with love, guilt, and loss, LaBelle poured out her heart to me, while I later discovered my tape recorder had not picked up a word. She generously did the interview a second time.

Finally, there was the afternoon with Jeanne White, the brave mother of her remarkable son, Ryan White, the boy from Kokomo, Indiana, who died of AIDS at age seventeen in 1990. That day, despite my best efforts at focusing my attention on the subject at hand, holding back my own emotions, I failed in this. With Jeanne White crying and remembering her last conversation with her son, I couldn't stop my own tears.

I hope you, too, will be touched by all this. Alas, a turning point does not have to be gloomy and there are many light moments here too. But I've learned more from the darkness than light, and believe that most people gain more wisdom from problems than solutions.

In the Epilogue, when all the notables are finished, I've included a final turning point from just an ordinary guy.

I hope that one day, when you're facing yet another turning point in your own life, something you read here might help, might comfort, might bring you closer to the child that lives within us all.

*New York*
September 1992

# ACKNOWLEDGMENTS

Heartfelt thanks to the therapists who have helped and loved me for the past twenty-two years. Exploring my own past has been the best preparation for understanding the lives of others.

Grateful thanks to my dearest friend Michael Simon, always there, wisely encouraging me to keep going.

Also, this book would not be possible were it not for former *New York Daily News* editor Gilman Spencer, who gave me the chance to write *Turning Point* and who always believed in me.

Equally kind and instrumental was the *New York Daily News*'s former publisher and chairman of the board Jim Hoge.

None of this would be possible without Jay Maeder, the brilliant magazine editor who carved out a special place for me at the *Daily News.*

Thanks also to my patient lawyer, Robert Youdelman, who puts up with my bossiness with such good-natured bemusement.

And special thanks to the persuasive Bill Goodstein, for his belief in the project.

I am also indebted to Brian Moss, my *Turning Point* editor at the *Daily News.*

And what would I do without friends like Gregory Barca, Scott Parris, Ed Nicholas, Walter Lumsby, Martin Lobenthal, my uncle, Dr. Richard Feinberg, Paul Huberdeau, Bunny Shestak, Jack "Jackster" La Fata Jr., and Pearl and Arthur Gleberman—Katie's keepers and my dearest breakfast pals.

And if she can hear me, to Nana, who always believed in me. I miss you every day.

Finally, one hundred twenty-two thank-yous to the men and women in this book who took the time to remember.

# He was a showbiz peon—the

Australian son of a gardener/ grocer who started singing at age fourteen—one half of an Everly-brotherish duo called the Allen Brothers. She, on the other hand, was a legend.

"And who would have guessed that *Judy Garland* would have bumped into *me,* in Hong Kong no less?" asked high-voltage songwriter-singer Peter Allen, reminiscing about the old days shortly before his death in June 1992.

Suffering from throat cancer and AIDS, Allen was bravely "Making Every Moment Count"—the title of his last RCA album—right up until the end, just as he made every moment count with Garland once upon a time.

"It was the strangest day—the real turning point of my life," Allen recalled of that time in May 1964. "I was working the Hong Kong Hilton with my partner (not actually my brother—I sang, he played guitar), and Judy was lying in a hospital bed with a tracheoto-my. She had just flown to the Orient from Australia—where she'd caused a scandal by braking concert dates.

"Garland's then-boyfriend, Mark Herron, heard me sing, and Judy got jealous of his having fun. Next night, she pulled a scarf around her neck and said: 'Let's

go.'" After, she asked the twenty-year-old Allen Brothers to become her opening act—'our big break'—a gig that lasted three years.

"She also asked me to meet her daughter Liza [Minnelli], who was then just eighteen—vibrant, wild, gorgeous. We were engaged within three weeks," and for the next three years, Allen lived with Minnelli while touring with Garland.

"Judy was like a great athlete, or circus act. She was petrified of audiences and ornery—had a physician hypnotizing her before concerts. Half the time, she wouldn't appear anyway. So Garland maniacs would attack the stage and grab us."

By the time Allen and Minnelli married in 1967, Garland was sliding downhill. "She'd lost her insane fight—against people, pills, audiences, the tax man—and when she finally gave up, the body just went." That was in 1969. In 1970, Allen's marriage collapsed, too.

"It was puppy love. . . .The Beatles had come in, my act was fizzling, I wanted to go off on my own as a songwriter, while Liza was getting raves for her nightclub act. I was miserable; she was booming. And that was hard for me. Both traveling, we just passed in the

night. One night, we looked at each other and both said: 'It's over.'" Garland and Minnelli gone in one fell swoop.

"I was freaked out, but oddly elated, too. For the first time in my life, I didn't have a partner, didn't have a wife. I was *free.*

"And out drowning my sorrows, I met [comic] David Steinberg, who liked my solo songs and asked me to be his opening act. So the day I left Liza, I became a singer-songwriter. Same day." The rest—signatures "Don't Cry Out Loud," "I Go to Rio," "I Honestly Love You," even Broadway flop *Legs Diamond*— brought Allen the fame he craved as a kid.

"The turn in the road that brought me to Judy and Liza," Allen reflected, "was ultimately the one that set me on my own way when I lost them both. I love them, both—always will."

Any regrets?

"Only one—not having a baby with Liza."

# PETER ALLEN

# By the time the flower

girl-turned princess had waltzed with Professor Higgins for the 2,717th and last time in *My Fair Lady* on Broadway in 1956, English beauty Julie Andrews had carved out a permanent place in entertainment history.

But despite her success, the actress, who next triumphed in *Camelot,* in 1960, had throughout her peculiar life held on to few close friends.

Although she was blessed with a sublime soprano and toured England singing operatic arias at age twelve, there was a darker side to the child prodigy, born Julia Elizabeth Welles in 1935, that kept her apart from others.

"My parents were both alcoholics," Julie Andrews remembers, "and I was a child freak with an adult voice at age eight, forced to grow up much too fast." The result left a gaping hole in her life: "I always had wished I'd had more family feeling," she confides, "and needed a good friend." So when a producer told her about a girl named Carol Burnett starring on Broadway in *Once Upon a Mattress,* a "blind date" was set up.

"Those arrangements are usually the kiss of death," Andrews laughs, "but our meeting was magical. I describe it as two kids who

suddenly discover they live on the same block.

"We both started performing as kids, we both came from alcoholic families, and we both had been caretakers, which is a tremendous burden for a kid. Being raised in a chaotic household, we were also both super-neat and super-square."

Over the years, the duo has appeared in three *Julie and Carol* TV specials; yet another, a thirtieth-anniversary show is planned for early 1993.

"Throughout all those years," Andrews says, "the things I first liked about Carol haven't changed a bit: She's ingenuous, she's straight, and she's real. When I was divorced years ago, Carol helped me; when she was divorced, I helped her. Kid problems and romance problems were always easier because we've had each other.

"Also, we regress and both become big kids when we're together—she's the lady and I'm the comedienne. But what comforts me the most in this dizzying world is that I know I can trust Carol completely. She's a sister to me and I love her a lot. I don't think anything could harm that relationship.

"And," Julie says, taking from her wrist an enamel-bangled bracelet lined with gold, "I treasure this, the most beautiful bracelet

I've ever seen. Carol hand-engraved the inside herself—'With Love.'"

# JULIE ANDREWS

# When Lucille Ball groggily

opened her eyes after heart surgery in April 1989, she attempted a few words with daughter Lucie Arnaz: "I asked the nurse to take off her oxygen mask," Arnaz recalls, "and Mom whispered, 'Wouldn't you know it. This was the day I was supposed to have my hair colored!'"

"We used to kiddingly call her the Henna Thud. She'd say, 'Oh, one day, honey, the Henna Thud will die and they won't have me to kick around anymore.'"

That day came April 26, 1989.

"It was 6:30 in the morning," says Arnaz, who was startled by the phone, answered by husband, actor Larry Luckinbill. "I could just tell something horrible had happened by the way Larry said, 'Yes, yes.' Then he turned to me: 'Your mother died.' Next thing I remember is flying through the air—I don't know how I left the bed—then sitting on the floor in the hallway slapping my face silly with both hands crying: 'No, no, no, no, no. I was in excruciating shock.'"

Lucie Arnaz was again ambushed by death, an-all-too-familiar presence in recent years.

"Talk about turning points," she groans. "In 1985, my dad's wife, Edie, my dearest friend, died of cancer. Then my maternal grand-mother died. Then, in 1986, my dad [Desi Arnaz] died of lung cancer. Then, six months after Mom died, the woman who literally raised me, Willie Mae Barker, died of a heart attack. And let's not even mention all my friends who have died from AIDS in the last five years—fifteen *close* friends."

The result for Arnaz was combat fatigue: "It was like war. I have felt a numbness about death, a numbness in life. I alternate between crying and wailing for thirty minutes nonstop; then other times just refusing to feel anything because I can't possibly take one more death.

"After covering up my feelings after my father died, I started therapy and discovered that my survival technique had always been putting up a big wall against feeling anything. To this day, it's hard for me to express any feeling other than humor and joy."

But she was able to work up anger at a TV movie-biography of her parents, *Lucy and Desi: Before the Laughter.*

"Total trash. If there is rein-carnation, both my mom and dad are going to come back and haunt CBS! Don't trust anybody (in show business). They're all scum!"

Happily, Arnaz says she's finally escaped the shadow of being the daughter of two TV legends.

"With all the love my mom gave me, she was a towering presence. I must say I felt some sense of relief the first year after she died—relieved not to constantly answer questions about her. That was debilitating and demeaning."

Now, she says with relief, "No more shadow. In fact, I once said if I ever wrote an autobiography it would be called, *Nothing Grows in the Shade!*"

# LUCIE ARNAZ

# "Oooooooh, easy, easy,

Charlie," Ed Asner coos, fumbling on hands and knees searching for the wristwatch just purloined by his two-and-a-half-year-old son, Charles Edward.

A daddy at sixty?

"Charlie," Asner blushes, "was not exactly a planned occurrence . . . he was a wonderful accident," a surprise package emerging, Asner says, from "an unbelievable string of circumstances"—actually a classic mid-life crisis that started back in 1981.

"I strayed," says the *Lou Grant* TV star, married twenty-eight years to wife Nancy before embarking first on an affair that resulted in a separation.

Then, with a divorce in the wind, Asner had another liaison, with a married talent coordinator at an L.A. radio station, named Carol Jean Vogelman.

"What happened first time around," Asner surmises, "was dictated by my unconscious. . . . That first affair was not designed to end my marriage." It did anyway. "I never thought divorce would happen to me. But there was no common ground in terms of sharing my involvement in politics and my union activism," says the die-hard liberal, former president of the Screen Actors Guild. "Nancy wasn't passionate about it."

Although Asner did discover a brief kind of passion with Vogelman, he not too long after found himself in an ugly court battle over child support with Vogelman's husband, who divorced his wife after Charlie's birth.

The press had a field day during seven months of medical tests and testimony: "There are still some scars. Her husband besmirched my name . . . though I always wanted to pay my rightful share. I love Charlie."

It was a fact initially resented by Asner's older children, twins Matthew and Liza, and Kate. "In earlier years, I had no magic or mystique for them as a father—I wasn't a buddy. Now I'm making a real effort."

The affair with Vogelman is long over. "I still love my ex-wife very much . . . and she's not bitter. We're tight, having dinner tonight. And Carol is the mother of my child and a friend." Very modern.

Would Asner, who says he "yearns for another chance at marriage," turn the clock back to 1986 to change things? "Absolutely not. If I hadn't had these problems, I might not have a wonderful new baby in my life. It's made me a better father to my older children, a better friend to my former wife, and I've discovered that the gruff-

ness my older kids understood as hot air won't work with Charlie. I treat him with kid gloves."

# ED ASNER

# Every single morning for

twenty years, the hyperkinetic actor would begin his day with seven cups of espresso, which infused him with enough energy to jog five miles before putting in nineteen-hour workdays.

"I was a workaholic of the worst kind," exclaims hearthrob actor Armand Assante, a self-professed addictive-personality type with a bedeviling affliction that nearly ended his life in 1987.

"For seven months in a row, I was working ninety hours a week and drinking an entire pot of coffee every morning," says the recent "Mambo King," then in the midst of back-to-back-to-back starring roles in *Hands of a Stranger, Napoleon and Josephine,* and *Jack the Ripper.*

On the *Ripper* set at London's Pinewood Studios in 1987, "I wasn't aware of feeling ill—not at all," he insists. "But poor diet, too much stress, and twenty years of drinking coffee had played tremendous havoc with my blood sugar. Coffee gave me an immediate high in the morning, then after working all day, I'd crash.

"One day, an actor literally died in my arms of a totally unexpected, cerebral hemorrhage," he remembers sadly. "He just fell over on top of me. That was a tremendous shock to my system."

The next day, after drinking a few glasses of wine, Assante collapsed in hypoglycemic shock, nearly dying himself. "I just fell over, blacked out," he recalls. "My doctor explained that when you're ingesting as much caffeine as I was, you literally force your pancreas to create huge quantities of insulin to combat the amount of blood sugar that you've introduced with coffee. I kept fainting for three weeks!"

For months, Assante, like any drug addict, faced a gruesomely painful rehabilitation. "Hellish, I'd call it. I stopped coffee cold turkey, felt intense anxiety, completely disoriented, and phenomenal exhaustion. Talk about drained. My system fell into complete havoc. I would sometimes sleep fifteen hours a day."

Four years later, Assante is a changed man. "I drank my first cup of decaf a few years ago, but mostly drink wonderful herbal teas that cleanse the system. I now walk ten to fifteen miles at a clip on weekends, I ride my horse twenty miles a day, my diet is 70 percent carbohydrate, 20 percent protein, and 10 percent fat."

Beyond the exercise and diet, Assante is more attentive to wife Karen and small daughters Anya and Alessandra.

No longer compulsively ambitious? "Nope. Going to a meeting and talking about a potential job bores the living daylights out of me. I get on my horse every morning and go off into the woods and just gallop," he says.

"Do anything," Assante recommends. "Pitch hay. Release endorphins. Read. Write. Be productive. But don't get caught up in compulsive pursuit."

# ARMAND ASSANTE

# *Gone With the Wind's* Belle

Watling, you'll recall, was just an old-fashioned hooker with scarlet curls and a heart of gold.

Her modern-day counterpart was a blond society gal, a descendant of *Mayflower* stock, with more business acumen than sexual desire.

"I didn't do *it*—I was the chief executive," explains Sydney Biddle Barrows, the rebellious blueblood dubbed the Mayflower Madam when busted in 1984 for running a three-hundred-girl Manhattan "escort service."

"Does Lee Iacocca stand on the assembly line? Selling sex didn't repulse me morally; it repulsed me physically, because I don't like strange people touching me."

Taking money, on the other hand, was a breeze. "Why not? Prostitution should absolutely be decriminalized. Let's get real: If you can give it away, why can't you sell it?

"We sell everything else. A man can go to his local watering hole, pour fifty dollars worth of drinks down a girl's throat, drag her upstairs, and hope she doesn't say no; or he can meet a gorgeous woman just showered, beautifully dressed, whose agenda is nothing but pleasing him. That's worth something."

And for five and a half years it was.

"Back then, I charged two hundred dollars per hour. I'd get forty percent, the girls sixty percent plus tips," until the day the vice squad grabbed seven thick notebooks of clients, shutting her down.

"Crack dealers and murderers don't go to jail," says Barrows. "Why should they save a bed for me? I turned myself in, pleaded guilty, paid a five-thousand-dollar fine, and wound up with a class D misdemeanor—same as a traffic ticket. It doesn't bother me—though my mother was horrified. Still, she's never said: 'How could you?' That's the way we do things in WASP homes. It doesn't exist if you don't talk about it."

But talk she does, lecturing women on techniques for pleasing their men—"Sixty percent of my clients were married men ignored by their wives"—and offering advice in *Mayflower Manners,* a sexual etiquette guide.

But, Barrows says, "I miss being in business and can't think of *anything* that would be as much fun as running an escort service."

She harbors no regrets. "None. I didn't do anything wrong. I didn't hurt anybody, I never revealed the names of clients, and

never will. And I helped college girls pay their rent.

"Monogamy as a practical reality," she finishes, "hasn't taken hold," though Madam herself wears a chastity belt.

"You have to go out with me six times before I will kiss you good night. 'Mayflower Madam' suits me: I really am prudish!"

# SYDNEY BIDDLE BARROWS

# Sailing in triumph past the

finish line, a winded, superbly conditioned Robby Benson patted himself on the back, for he had conquered the grueling 26 miles and 385 yards of the 1983 New York Marathon in just three hours and five minutes.

But shortly thereafter, the then-twenty-six-year-old actor began to feel like a sixty-year-old man.

"I was exhausted *all the time,*" he recalls, "had shortness of breath, dizziness—all the classic symptoms" of a man born with a heart problem, an aortic valve defect.

"There are," Benson explains, "three leaflets that open and close on the aortic valve and I was born with two."

Essentially, that means the heart leaks. "I never took it seriously," though the results of a battery of EKGs and other tests in 1984 changed all that.

"I was told I had to have open-heart surgery for a valve replacement . . . that they would split open my chest, take my heart out. . . . "

Benson didn't even flinch: "I had no fear, I never panic, I was born a jock and the jock just *took over.* I wouldn't allow myself to be afraid.

"But"—Benson grins—"I have a personality trait that's comic: Right afterward I fall apart!"

Exiting the hospital just four days after surgery and back at the gym in two weeks, Benson began to think.

"About my own vulnerability," he says. "I used to think I could do anything, but suddenly I realized I wasn't invincible. My own mortality became an issue coupled with new life—the miracle of having a baby," daughter Lyric. "I didn't want to miss it all, not even a second," and he doesn't.

"I have a bovine valve, so now I moo in the morning," he jokes about his replacement part provided by a cow. "Isn't that wild? I'm playing ball again. But I also realize I could die. I understand that very well. Life is very fragil . . . and the cow's valve will eventually need to be replaced.

"I think about it *constantly.* Life is a thin thread. I've learned that you can't take anything for granted, that we all have to live with uncertainties, that the world is a fast, frightening place."

# ROBBY BENSON

# Lately, you just can't miss

the blond curls and muskily sweet voice of New Haven-born Michael Bolton, rockin' and poppin' on MTV with "Love Is a Wonderful Thing," the hit single featured on Bolton's Columbia album, *Time, Love and Tenderness.*

But for a former hard rocker who struggled for sixteen years in relative obscurity until 1987's hit "That's What Love Is All About," what were the chances he'd become 1990's Grammy winner for Best Pop Vocal or that he'd attain the No. 1 spot on *Billboard*'s pop singles chart?

"Nonexistent," laughs the handsome near-forty-year-old, who recounts the painful "great ascent" from rock to pop-soul.

An athletic kid who idolized Smokey Robinson, Marvin Gaye, and Stevie Wonder, Bolton recalls he started "singing at five, performing and writing my own songs with four chords and a cheapo guitar at twelve," and signing his first record deal with Epic at fifteen.

But during the seventies, his jabs at hard rock never brought stardom, "to put it mildly," he says, smiling. "Nothing happened! I was always asking myself, 'Where's my edge, my power?' It took me almost ten years to realize I shouldn't be focusing on what I *thought* was the edge—rock music. Instead I was

neglecting my strength—R&B soul elements and emotional themes.

"I was down," says Bolton. His checks were bouncing and his wife, Maureen, and daughters, Isa, Holly, and Taryn, were facing eviction. "It was as dark as it gets," he says, until 1982, when manager Louis Levin took the reins of Bolton's career, convincing him to write pop songs. Streisand, Cher, Kenny Rogers, The Pointer Sisters, and Kiss lapped up the hits Bolton created.

"If there's a turning point to this story, that's it. Louis believed in me, got me a deal with CBS, and soon enough I dropped my resistance, dropped my 'edge' theory, and started singing those pop songs *myself.*

"My R&B roots saved me," he says, but not his marriage. Love may be a wonderful thing to some, but Bolton recently signed the dotted line on his divorce. "A done deal," he grimaces.

"The starting-over story is happening for me. There is a freeing, promising, positive feeling when something ends that shouldn't continue. I want to fall in love again, I want to get into acting in films. That's the next turning point—the world opening up for me, getting really bright."

# MICHAEL BOLTON

# Like crusty Emma Harte—the

driven heroine in *A Woman of Substance* who rises from humble beginnings to found a business empire—novelist Barbara Taylor Bradford has achieved much the same rags-to-riches stardom by sheer force of will.

An only child born in 1933 to Winston and Freda Taylor, a machinery engineer and a nurse in Leeds, England, the tomboyish Barbara was always "falling out of trees," she laughs, as she gobbled up all of Dickens and dreamed about becoming a writer herself.

At eleven, she made her first sale. "That," she recalls, "was my first turning point—when I *knew* I was going to be a writer. I wrote a story about Sally and her little pony and sold it to a magazine for seven-pounds-six. My destiny was sealed."

The girl brazenly quit high school at sixteen, bought a trench coat, and joined the typing pool at the *Yorkshire Evening Post,* ignoring her parents' wish that she attend Leeds University.

"Mum and Dad shrugged their shoulders: 'Oh my God, no! You've got to go to school.' But I thought that would be *silly*—that I couldn't learn to be a writer there, so I made a deal with my mother. If I didn't like the newspaper job after six months, I'd go back to school."

She never did. A cub reporter in 1950 at age seventeen, women's page editor at eighteen, Bradford joined the *London Evening News* at twenty, rolling out stories on fashion, show business, and crime.

In 1964, she and her husband of three years, film producer Bob Bradford, moved to New York City. For the next twelve years, Barbara Bradford wrote an interior design column, dreaming of one day fulfilling her childhood dream of becoming a novelist. "Over the years, I made four attempts at suspense novels but lost my nerve each time and never finished one. Fear of failure."

Finally, in 1976, she hatched an idea about a woman of substance. "'This is it!' I told my husband. 'I'm forty-two years old and I want to fulfill that childhood dream—I'm going to start a novel and finish one!' Within a few hours I had the whole sixty-four years of Emma Harte's story in my head.

"The whole world loves a survivor," says the queen of the romantic saga, "someone who uses adversity to make herself stronger. I put emotion on paper well."

Did she ever. The 1,520-page, 16 1/2-pound manuscript, published in 1979, was an overnight bestseller, spawning Harte sequels and TV miniseries for

each successive book—*Hold the Dream, To Be the Best, Voice of the Heart, Act of Will, The Women in His Life, Remember,* etc.

The superstar author coasts on a $25 million contract with HarperCollins, her childhood dream a reality with over 35 million books in print.

"I tell a good story," she merrily shrugs.

# BARBARA TAYLOR BRADFORD

# Soul mates giggling over

dinner, that's what they were. Goldie Hawn and Eileen Brennan—best friends since *Private Benjamin* invigorated their careers back in 1980—were hugging goodbye outside a restaurant in Venice, Calif. . . .

"One minute I was laughing with Goldie at her car," Brennan recalls, "and the next thing I knew, I was propelled right into a wonderfully blissful white light." It was the light of death. Brennan had just been mowed down by a car that October 27, 1982.

"But I remember nothing," says Brennan, of that horrible moment. "Goldie says I looked dead. Nobody expected me to live."

Brennan suffered massive internal bleeding, had both legs crushed, nose broken, skull and facial bones fractured, and an eyeball wrenched from its socket. But three days later, the actress miraculously awakened.

"Imagine," she exclaims, "coming out of this place of enormous peace beyond any words and waking up to *excruciating* agony." Only narcotics were able to ease the pain.

Brennan returned home three months later, her new TV series, *Private Benjamin,* canceled: "I was in shock. And furious. I saw no point in living. My spirit was dead, dead,

dead. My legs were crippled. My career was destroyed. Although I never consciously considered suicide, subliminally, I no longer cared.

"But humor is the sound of God," she says, "and my kids [Sam and Patrick] pointed out the cosmic humor, the absurdity of my being at the height—making thirty thousand dollars a week as a single parent—and then having it blown away by going out to dinner."

Learning to walk again, Brennan remained hooked on painkillers and deeply depressed until 1984. Acupuncture, biofeedback, and psychiatry couldn't heal her emotional scars, until . . .

"The real turning point, entering the Betty Ford Center. I was almost spiritually bankrupt. But I found that self-pity was a destructive force, blaming everybody else. I saw that I had control over my own thoughts and that thoughts are power.

"Suddenly, the veil was ripped off, and my life was put right back in my lap. I said: 'It's up to you, baby. You can *do* it.'"

And she did. As for her still creaky legs and the pain, she says, "I don't give a damn about it anymore. It doesn't mean anything. I do just the opposite of what my 'lower' self tells me to do—which is

to bitch and moan and grab a dish of Häagen-Dazs.

"Instead, I work out, I take the dogs and walk, I do anything to be positive."

Today, calling her accident "a paradoxical gift," Brennan believes "there are missions in life—and this was mine. A turning point is something that takes a whole lifetime to understand. You never know when it's going to hit you, but you better keep your eyes open."

# EILEEN BRENNAN

# Leaving the stage of the Sands

Hotel in Las Vegas, the young comedian was barely able to walk. He collapsed in his dressing room, frantically swallowing three extra-strength aspirins for unbearable back pain.

"I was a wreck . . . if my body were a building, they would have razed it," jokes David Brenner, remembering back to 1974 when he suffered from a Pandora's box of physical ailments: double scoliosis of the spine, a herniated disk, sciatica in both legs, and a degenerative disease of ten vertebrae, not to mention bone spurs pinching the nerves of his lower back.

"Back then, I was in pain twenty-four hours a day, and on such heavy painkillers I didn't know who I was."

Headed toward a wheelchair by age thirty, the funny man visited more than sixty orthopedic surgeons, chiropractors, massage therapists, biofeedback pros and acupuncturists—and, he says, "I didn't get five minutes of relief from anybody."

In a last-ditch effort, Brenner, on the advice of Sonny Bono, a fellow back sufferer, consulted the unorthodox Dr. Milton Reder of Manhattan, now deceased, who became infamous for treating patients suffering from severe back pain with medical cocaine adminis-

tered through the nose, until he was forbidden to do so by the New York State Department of Health.

"Dr. Reder," Brenner explains, "took Q-tip applicators, dipped them in a ten percent solution of *medical* cocaine and then anesthetized the sphenopalatine ganglion, a supersensitive area at the top of the nose, which controls pain throughout the body.

"My medical condition remained the same, but all the agony from pinched nerves and lower back pain suddenly disappeared."

Brenner dismisses detractors who says his positive results were attributable simply to his being high on cocaine. "I was involved in drugs just like anybody else," he says, "and I can tell you from my own experience that using cocaine does not help a troubled back."

Now pain-free, Brenner is ecstatic: "Everybody has disabilities, but you gotta fight back. I sail, I snow-ski, I run and I even lift weights," this from the born-again athlete who starred in *The David Brenner I Hate to Work Out Workout.*

"I always looked real thin and puny, but in the last two years I've been able to beef up and enjoy my life. I'm really on the upswing: no pain, lots of weights and a new book out."

Where does he get all his spunk?

"From Burt Lancaster," he says. "In one of his movies, he offers his son advice: 'You gotta live your life up bold.' I never forgot that."

# DAVID BRENNER

# For weary Christmas shoppers

running out of ideas, time, or money, how about a scented chintz teddy bear from Saks, a strawberry-shaped needlepoint kit from Bloomie's, wildly flowered glazed chintz slipcovers from Macy's, or Christmas bells stuffed with spicy potpourri from Lord & Taylor?

"Anything that makes a room feel cozier sounds right to me," exclaims interior designer Mario Buatta, the chintz-crazed mastermind of such affordable home furnishings. The zany Buatta whips up yards of swags, bows, ruffles, tassels, and painted wooden bells for high-profile customers like Barbara Walters, the Forbeses, Barbara Bush, and Billy Joel, who is Buattafying "a nice three-bedroom townhouse," he says, "for about $1 million."

Not bad money for an Italian boy from Staten Island with an exotic name. Born October 20, 1935, little Mario was raised glamorously by society orchestra conductor Felix Buatta in a glass, steel, and chrome house.

"That's why I *despise* modern decoration," exclaims Buatta, who regrets not being able to make foot or fingerprints on the tables and carpets.

After bored stints in architecture at Staten Island's Wagner College and Manhattan's Cooper Union, Mario worked at B. Altman until apprenticing abroad, where he scoured English country homes, "inhaling seven-generation lifestyles."

Transplanting his version of the English look to America, Buatta opened his own business in April 1963, at age twenty-seven.

But disaster struck in July that year. "*My* whole life stopped *cold* just at the point everything was progressing so well," he remembers.

"I had been working seven days a week on my first job, the offices of the New York World's Fair, feeling very weak, weird, and nauseous. I saw three doctors who diagnosed it as fatigue. Then one night, I woke up and my whole body felt like it was exploding inside . . . terrific pain and my abdomen swelled. That's all I remember. . . .

"I later found out my appendix had burst ten days earlier. I was taken to the hospital and fell into a very deep coma. I was given last rites three times.

"But three days later I literally awoke from the dead," he says, "and over the next two months of recovering, felt transformed. You see, up until then, my life had unfolded relatively easily. But faced with death, I felt an incredible surge of restless energy that has never left me."

At age fifty-seven, with 120 decorating jobs on the books and dozens of licensed home furnishings by Aromatique—"only chintz linoleum is missing"—life is sweet. "I got a second chance and I've learned that the whole joy of living is loving what you do and working hard at it. You can never stop and never should. That's death's job."

# MARIO BUATTA

# The somber child with "droopy

Burnett eyes," stringy brown hair, and buck teeth overheard her curvaceous mother, Louise, profess that "Carol's a *real* Burnett."

"That means homely," the girl whispered to herself, secretly maddened by her absentee parents.

"Both Daddy and Mom," Carol Burnett recalls, "were drunks—*couldn't* stop themselves," so the disheartened seven-year-old, who lived with her "Nanny" in a $35-a-month flat on welfare, would ask her divorced parents over and over: "Do you love me?"

"They would say yes," Burnett says, "and I would answer: 'Then, if you love me, *don't drink.'* But they drank anyway, and I thought they didn't love me."

Then hope appeared: "When I was ten," remembers Burnett, "my dad's mother contracted leukemia. And he promised her that, as long as she was alive, he would never drink again. For an entire year, Daddy was on the wagon, and I was ecstatic."

Then shattered. "When Daddy's mother finally died, he came over to Nanny's, told me he had had 'a few beers' after his mother's funeral. This was the low point of my life. My heart felt like lead. A few hours later, I found him lying on the floor unconscious. I thought

he might be dead. But he was just drunk. Then I became livid and hysterical. I socked him with my fist right in his face, really hard—again and again," and the hysterical girl had to be pulled off her father.

Even years later, when twenty-one-year-old Burnett saw her forty-six-year-old father, Jody, dying in a charity hospital with tuberculosis—"I was crying, telling him I wanted to be an actress"—she had not yet recovered from that fateful day so many years before.

"But then, just seven years ago," Carol smiles, the year she started writing a diary, "I realized Daddy really did love me, that he couldn't help himself, that he had a disease that could have been treated."

Three daughters and one divorced husband later, "I have finally stopped laying an 'ugly trip' on myself," says Burnett, who divides her time between L.A. and Maui.

"In my recent show—*Carol & Company*—each week I played a different comedic character, but not one of them had a hangup about being ugly. That's an awful thing to live with and it's taken me years to recover from it. Even during the days of my TV series, I was always putting myself down to get a laugh. Nowadays," she says, "my

consciousness is raised through yoga, and I know, deep inside me, I'm a mature woman, a mother, and I'm not going to do that anymore."

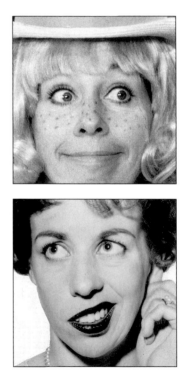

# CAROL BURNETT

# The pugnacious hell-raiser

from Goose Creek, Texas—nick-named Teddy Jack Eddy—was a rock-'n'-rollin' football jock with an appetite for trouble.

"My motto was 'Reckless Momentum,'" grins actor Gary Busey, describing his Teddy Jack Eddy persona as "a heat-seeking missile with a huge smile."

Born June 29, 1944, the part-American Indian, part-Irish boy suffered "from attention-deficit disorder (lack of parental nurturing)," he says.

The result was rock-bottom self-esteem: "With buck teeth, big eyes, a huge mouth, and skinny legs, I was just trying to break even," Busey laughs. But he excelled in football and theater at Kansas State and Oklahoma State: "My ability to keep the bad guys laughing was the key to my survivability," he believes. Barely surviving in Hollywood, Busey dabbled in ten nondescript films before pinning down an Academy Award nomination for his riveting title performance in *The Buddy Holly Story* (1978). But afterward, he says, "frightened of success I felt I didn't deserve," the panicked actor turned to cocaine and alcohol. "It became a vicious cycle. My career wasn't moving, I couldn't live without cocaine."

Blimped out at 240 pounds—"I looked like a potato in a leotard"—Busey hit bottom in June 1985. "I finally went inside myself," he says, "and a psychiatrist eased me off coke."

By this point, Busey's fifteen-year marriage to Judy was kaput: "She had rightly turned her back on me to escape the reckless momentum of my life." That reckless moment surfaced yet again on December 4, 1988, when the avid motorcyclist nearly lost his life taking "a ticket to hell," he says.

"I was accelerating around a corner at forty miles an hour—too fast," and hitting the cement with the right side of his head, Busey required two hours of neurosurgery at Cedars-Sinai Medical Center to remove blood clots between a fractured skull and the crucial right side of his brain. Unable to walk, talk, or even swallow, he lapsed into seven weeks of posttraumatic amnesia, though he does remember a visit from the Grim Reaper: "He was Death, with a message from the higher forces: 'Relax,' he said, 'It's not your time to die, so why try to kill yourself? You have been given gifts at birth that you are now ready to receive.'

"I had a ninety-eight percent chance of never coming back full, but I've come back better than

full," says the actor, who benefits from acupuncture, reflexology, and weight-training.

"The head injury opened me up to my deeper self by knocking away two-thirds of my defensive armor," Busey says. "The accident was a godsend, warning me to stop and get my life in order. I realize I don't need to be angry or aggressive, or goal-oriented anymore. I just need to be me—as cleanly, as gently, as calmly as I can be. Now I'm more fine-tuned."

# GARY BUSEY

39

# The one-man comedy factory—

which furiously wrote, produced, and directed a live, ninety-minute weekly show for eight solid years—was hopelessly overstimulated. An overload of adrenaline and insecurity made sleep impossible. Sid Caesar turned to drugs.

"The Scotch and sleeping pills were overlapping," says the legendary TV star, remembering the slow decline of his comedic splendor circa 1958, the year *Caesar's Hour* was canceled and a twenty-year nightmare began.

"What do I do?" Caesar cried. "Where do I go? What do I say? Why me?"

"The big black blob began," he explains, referring to a cycle of depression, guilt, self-punishment, and fear of financial ruin.

"I was angry, depressed, and wanted to blot out the pain. . . . I binged for the next twenty years. Before getting on planes, I'd swallow six tranquilizers and two sleeping pills and wash them down with booze. I usually passed out in the air."

On the ground, he tortured his family with his belligerent, suicidal tantrums. Wife Florence says he was a sadistic, lunatic driver. Children Rick, Michele, and Karen witnessed the growth of an irrational, sarcastic, schizoid monster.

By 1978, Caesar had also become agoraphobic ("terrified to go anywhere or do anything"), finally bottoming out with a nervous breakdown and a hospital detox program.

"I didn't have the strength anymore to go on as I had," he whispers. "I actually looked in the mirror: *'Sid, do you want to live or do you want to die?'* It was that simple."

That same year Caesar's ultimate salvation came with the purchase of a cassette tape recorder. "I became my own father, my own doctor," he recalls, "by talking to myself and *listening* to the tapes."

Caesar conducted dialogues between "Sid" (his nurturing parent side) and "Sidney" (the addict).

"So you want to take a drink, Sidney? You idiot! You stupid *schlemiel!* Why the hell are you even thinking like this? . . . Let yourself enjoy a meal, a cigar, let yourself alone. . . ."

For six months, the talks continued, "and I finally realized I *deserved* a career, *deserved* to have friends, people who love me. I had made friends with *myself.*"

Nowadays, "I still begin every morning with a long walk and a long talk . . . and I cure myself every day," says the near-seventy comic.

Notice the muscles: "Each morning, I walk four miles, do 300 situps, 150 pushups, 80 chinups and 150 curls."

If you miss him on TV or in nightclubs, catch him in Central Park, where I left him, tape-recording away on cassette No. 105, twelve years after he started.

". . . It's a beautiful day. . . . Appreciate life. . . . Enjoy, enjoy. . . .

"Love you . . . ."

# SID CAESAR

# Rather than birthday cake and

balloons, Maurice Joseph Micklewhite Jr., better known as Michael Caine, rang in his fortieth birthday with a funeral dirge of depressive thoughts, a foggy gloom relieved only by the soothing stupor of alcohol.

The roguish British star was, back then, shocked to discover that the fame of *Alfie* and *The Ipcress File* had brought him nothing but misery.

"Women were hanging on to me. I was extreme, wild, very dissolute—late nights, parties, well on my way to becoming an alcoholic," says Caine, who had seen millions come his way so easily.

"My father, on the other hand, never had time to enjoy life," adds Caine. The senior Micklewhite "schlepped iced fish" at the Billingsgate Fish Market in the heart of London's Depression, and Caine's mother was a charlady.

"But I never knew we were poor, and thought *everybody* ate tinned corned beef instead of ham."

By the early seventies, Caine's cupboard was stocked full, yet he was spiritually running on empty. Then, while glumly watching a Maxwell House coffee commercial the day after his fortieth birthday, onto the screen strode the former Miss World contestant Shakira Baksh.

"The absolutely *last* thing I wanted was a wife," says the actor, who was nonetheless tantalized by the 1973 commercial featuring Shakira.

"I fell in love *instantly* and flew to Rio, then to London, where I finally tracked her down. Her flatmates immediately nicknamed me 'The White Shark' because they were familiar with my womanizing reputation. She was brave and went out with me anyway."

Brave indeed. "Shakira had been blown up in the Guyanan Revolution when she was eighteen; her face was horribly burned, but surgeons refused to perform skin grafts. She swam every day in the sea, and the saltwater healed her. I loved her bravery."

Years later, fashion-plate Shakira, a grown daughter Natasha, and Caine are rock-solid.

The secret?

"Total commitment. I concentrate on her like I concentrate on movie acting. I call it the laser technique. Zoom." Also: "I'm monogamous," says the former playboy, who has made more than sixty films. "That's because I know what's out there."

"Sex," Caine tells me in parting, "stays interesting if you delve deeper and deeper into *one* relationship. I've discovered lots of different women inside Shakira . . . so it's not boring. If you've seen my wife, you know what I'm talking about."

# MICHAEL CAINE

# "When you're born into show

business at a very early age to parents who know nothing about the industry, you don't get the emotional support you need," muses Diahann Carroll.

Disastrously married three times, almost married to Sidney Poitier and David Frost, and now reunited with estranged fourth husband Vic Damone, emotional support is something she values.

"My parents," Carroll says, "were loving, but not equipped to deal with my fame—which frightened and awed them, so they weren't very terribly helpful."

Left on her own, the singer-actress soared professionally but sank otherwise, first in a breezy marriage to casting director Monte Kay, father of her daughter, Suzanne.

"I was young, he was young, and we weren't in love," so she left him for a nine-year affair with Sidney Poitier.

"That was a true love affair, but he refused to divorce his wife. It was: 'I'm unhappy at home, my wife doesn't understand me, I'm getting a divorce.' And I believed it—until I finally ended it.

"That was the start of a turning point. In analysis, I saw that Sidney was a dead end, horrible for my self-esteem. I felt I deserved more," which included a three-year affair with David Frost.

"Incompatibility covers a lot of ground. A lovely man, but grossly self-involved—which made me uncomfortable. So I broke it off."

Carroll next eloped with a Las Vegas boutique owner who beat her, the marriage crumbling in just four months. "I take the fifth on that one, still wasn't responsible for my behavior—literally didn't know what I was doing."

Even worse, in 1975 Carroll married "a moody young genius, a very manipulative, strange young man fifteen years my junior," a *Jet* magazine editor who died intoxicated in a car crash less than two years later. "Drove off a cliff, maybe a suicide. Something right out of *Dynasty*," says Carroll, convinced he was after her money.

Carroll finally surrendered her compulsive craving for a marriage license: "Finally, at last, if there was one thing I understood, it was that I didn't know how to select a partner. Period. So for the next ten years, I dated but stayed single—vowed never to marry again, until I met Mr. Damone."

# DIAHANN CARROLL

# The slaphappy comedian who hit

the big time on *Caesar's Hour*, and on Red Buttons's and Danny Thomas's shows once called herself the "dowager queen" of the TV quiz, comedy, and variety-show circuit.

Her name was Pat Carroll, and she was a go-anywhere, do-anything clown armed with forty-three years' experience, a disarming chuckle and a razor-blade wit.

This was money in the bank until January 2, 1975, the day her divorce from theatrical agent Lee Karsian was finalized.

"That's when I discovered that nobody wanted a fat lady with bad legs," says the bubbly actress, still dimpled and grateful that she survived her gruesome change of life.

"Everything went sour and negative at once: There I was—after twenty years of marriage—divorced, unemployed, and raising three kids in high school," Sean, Kerry, and Tara.

Her situation worsened in 1976 when knee surgery disabled the actress: "The . . . little padding in my right knee where the two joints come together was shattered after forty-two years of pratfalls. Suddenly I was in horrible, excruciating pain. I'll have a baby any day of the week—but that kind of pain I never want again. I realized the

leg ain't ever going to be right again and felt relegated to actor's purgatory—disabled and waiting for the phone to ring."

Overweight, depressed, and graduating from crutches to a cane, Carroll says she healed herself with positive thinking. "Rather than sitting and moaning, I began thinking and plotting," she remembers. "'Come on, girl, get yourself together,' I told myself. 'What are we going to do with our life?' I'm Irish-stubborn and do believe all of us have a reason for being here; we just have to find it."

Fueled by her "original passion for the serious theater . . . something to feed my soul," and tired of TV, she became fascinated by the life of expatriate American writer Gertrude Stein. In 1979, she bravely unveiled her *Gertrude Stein Gertrude Stein Gertrude Stein*, a virtuoso one-woman show that won her a Grammy, a Drama Desk Award, and an Outer Critics Circle Award, proving she could reshape her image.

"If you don't see yourself in a different light, nobody else will," says the actress, who has since tackled such roles as the nurse in *Romeo and Juliet* and, last year, she appeared in *The Merry Wives of Windsor*.

"I learned when you're at the bottom of the well, if you can hang onto the bucket, somebody's going to pull it up."

Who? "Me. I listened to the five-year-old child inside me—Patsy Anne, who wanted to have fun. The lesson was that nobody else can be responsible for you but you. I didn't wait for a miracle. If I hadn't had that horrible surgery and a failed marriage, I would never have tested myself. It's never too late, and you're never too old."

# PAT CARROLL

# The gangly gal from San

Francisco was an only child with huge brown eyes and a passion for Daddy. Every night she sat transfixed while her father—Christian Science lecturer/newspaper editor George Channing—taught her rhythmic spirituals.

Then, before bedtime, the girl's mother, Adelaide, would lecture the overly tall girl to act "petite" in school, to blend in, but little Carol became the class clown instead. She hit the big time in fourth grade.

"That was the actual turning point of my life—the first time my life had meaning to me," exclaims comedienne Carol Channing, remembering her early days at Commodore Sloat Elementary School, the moment her gift for mimicry first took flight.

"A boy in my class, Bobby Schmaltz—like herring—nominated me for secretary of the student body. I was supposed to get up onstage and tell the kids why they should vote for me. My knees shaking, I couldn't think of one reason why they *should*—so I started imitating Miss Bernard, the principal of our school, a forerunner to Julia Child: 'Go to the polls and vote for Carol,' I mugged. Then I did Mr. Shruggs, the chemistry teacher—who blew up the classroom once a term. Then I did Marjorie Gould—

the cutest girl in the class—swinging her fanny around."

Soon enough, Channing was basking in a sea of laughter. "My God," she exclaims, "it was holy chaos! But I had a safe, warm feeling, the euphoria of being on stage and communicating with people. A bomb could have dropped, and it didn't matter, because we were all together.

"Suddenly, I realized we're all alike! What I saw in Mr. Shruggs, they saw. We all laugh at the same things and fall in love with the same things. I was no longer an only child. I was no longer lonely. That was a great feeling. I was a part of the human race. From then on I knew exactly where I was going.

"I went home and told my father, my confidant, what a wonderful thing had happened. 'Now, let me tell you an old French adage,' he said. 'Be careful what you set your heart upon, for you shall surely get it.'"

And she did. She studied drama and dance at Bennington College, and then eventually captured stardom in what became her signature roles of Lorelei Lee in *Gentlemen Prefer Blondes* (1949), and Dolly Levi in *Hello, Dolly!* (1964). More recently she toured the nation in a one-woman show while push-

ing her "Broadway Collection" of jewelry (advertised on the QVC home shopping network).

But nothing, she insists, was more thrilling than her fourth-grade debut.

"That very day," she concludes, "I asked my father a question. 'You mean I can lay down my life right now and decide to become an actress?' He nodded his head. And I said, "Then that's it. I'll starve, I'll go across the desert with no water, anything.' Luckily, I didn't die of thirst!"

# CAROL CHANNING

# "I'm having a *mid-life crisis*,"

booms the ever-controversial Cher, emerging into the spring air after a hibernation of eighteen celibate months. Besieged through the end of 1991, Cher battled Epstein-Barr (chronic fatigue syndrome), fought off pneumonia, and survived a breakup with Bon Jovi guitarist Richie Sambora. Not to mention a stalled movie career and the super-market-tabloid barracudas.

Cooking with gas once again, the diva has pulled herself back to health with exotic herbs and home-opathic remedies—and she's reassessing everything.

Like her duplex on lower Broadway: "It was getting too rough downtown," she says, "and I don't *have* that kind of *fight* in me anymore." Malibu and Aspen are becoming her new venues.

Her career: "I'm *not* sure if I want to continue to be Cher," she muses. "Too limiting. What if I wanted to become a lawyer or a doctor?"

Heat-seeking missiles like former-loves Rob Camilleti (an aspiring actor, former bagel maker) and Sambora: "Loneliness is not the worst thing that can happen to you," she surmises.

Cher also used to think her two children, Chastity Bono and Elijah Blue Allman were enough.

"But I'd consider having another baby in a heartbeat," she says.

And video-record-concert-movie Cher used to work around the clock; but "I'm getting *older*. Now I'm learning how to *pace* myself."

*Mmmmm.* The blossoming maturity and newfound serenity, she says, results from being roman-tically unattached and accepting the ravages of Epstein-Barr—bat-tling swollen lymph nodes, headaches, chills, muscle pain, plus the pneumonia last December:

"I was really, really sick, wor-ried, and really, really frightened," she whispers. "It was rough. My doctor put me on lots of Japanese and German herbs, and massive amounts of vitamin C," none of which battles depression: "Well, I've gone through that a lot too, but I know being tired or depressed won't last forever. I can kinda will it away, just keep going through it and working out helps." A boyfriend was the only remedy not required. She laughs: "Actually not being with anyone for eighteen months was refreshing, a really lib-erating experience. Most of the time I wasn't lonely." Will there be any husbands succeeding Sonny Bono and Gregg Allman? "At one time, I wanted to marry Robert [Camiletti] *really* badly but he

needed time to go off and find him-self. And Richie [Sambora] was like trying to hit a moving target. When he was ready, I wasn't."

Still vulnerable to love? "Absolutely. God, if I lost that, I would feel terrible, but if you just jump into just anything, anything is what you get."

Finally out of hibernation? "Actually I'm not. For me, it's good to go *into* hibernation, even if I'm not sick, because the lights are too hot being in the public eye. Oliver Stone asked me why I stopped making movies, and I said I needed to cool down. I needed to come in and get close to myself. And that's exactly where I am—close to myself—and it feels great."

# CHER

# Old anchormen, you see, don't

fade away," Walter Cronkite intoned sentimentally, as he handed over his baby—the *CBS Evening News*—to Dan Rather. "They just keep coming back for more. And that's the way it is, Friday, March 5, 1981."

The way it was *supposed* to be. But, Cronkite explains, "making documentaries and playing a major role covering presidential elections," as he expected, is not the way it turned out.

"It was"—Cronkite gulps— "unfortunate that CBS did not live up to what had been promised. That first year out I got exclusives with a number of world leaders, none of which CBS ever broadcast."

Why not? "There's only one star at a time and they had to build up Dan, but why it's gone on so long, I don't know. Dan's strength is being in the field—he's terribly good at that." Alas, withering himself in left field, a disgruntled Cronkite has grumbled for years over his fading star at CBS, and his forced retirement last year from the network's board of directors is yet another symbol that his life has unalterably moved from the high wire down to the net.

"Three of us over age seventy have been phased over and out." He smiles, musing on a decade-long transition that has left him increasingly cynical.

"At first, I felt a great release. I never was depressed, because I was tired of the daily grind. I wanted to step down when I was sixty-five and enjoy life—sail around the world in between hosting thirteen episodes of *Universe.* "

But after two seasons, Cronkite's *Universe* shrank like bad cotton, his assignments dwindling to ceremonial spots, though CBS continued to pay him $1 million a year. "It wasn't ageism at the beginning," says Cronkite, now seventy-five. "I don't blame them for wanting a younger look, though there's plenty of youthful vigor left in me. I make speeches, documentaries here and there, write a thousand words on the Middle East, you name it. Plenty to do. I feel terribly sad for people who reach advanced age without having other interests. . . . Those are the tragic figures, not me."

Cronkite says his passion for sailing and the stability of a fifty-year-plus marriage to Betsy have provided him the solace he has needed.

"In the last ten years, when I sail and leave civilization and return to a primordial atmosphere of wind and sea and air and sky, I feel completely refreshed. I can forget any-

thing that's bothering me. Then I come home to a wife who does not take herself, life, or me very seriously. That's the secret of my marriage—having a wife with an advanced sense of humor. We can both laugh about everything, including some of the disappointments over at CBS."

A relaxed Cronkite is asked if he's bitter. Long pause. "I'd rather not go into detailed psychoanalysis." And that's the way it is.

# WALTER CRONKITE

# She was just another twenty-

six-year-old New Jersey housewife, accustomed to nothing more than modest means, busy tending the home and five kids—but every morning she was up at five, working at the kitchen table, doggedly pursuing a private dream: Someday she was going to be a successful writer.

"Honey," her husband cooed, watching her bent over the Formica kitchen table, "think of it just as a hobby."

She agreed.

So how, then, did suspense queen Mary Higgins Clarke carve out a kingdom, one which includes a $11.4 million record-breaking contract with Simon & Schuster, making her the highest-paid female mystery writer in the world? "I *knew* I'd be a writer from age seven onward," Clarke says, though it was adversity that put her on the mystery map.

The story begins in 1939, when, at twelve, she fell in love with a college boy named Warren. She married him ten years later. A perfect union: "Just about. But he smoked three packs a day, and I was merrily serving bacon and eggs, steaks. . . . In 1962, he had a major heart attack. In 1964, after a second, he was just home a week when the third one killed him. I was thirty-six and had five kids, a mort-

gaged $13,000 house and three $10,000 insurance policies. That was it."

Suddenly the housewife couldn't afford to call her hobby a hobby anymore. "I *had* to work. I began writing radio scripts, twenty dollars a script, one hundred dollars a week." A 1969 biography of George Washington flopped, but that same year a red light blinked.

"Indeed," Clarke smiles, "I looked over my bookcase at the mysteries I loved, and my hunch was that I should *write* what I loved to *read*. I followed that hunch." The result: the 1975 bestseller *Where Are the Children?*, a terrifying tale of a childnapper. "I knew," she says, "that any time a child is missing, the whole world cares."

The whole world did. Today it's 15 million copies of her books later: *A Stranger Is Watching, The Cradle Will Fall, Stillwatch, While My Pretty One Sleeps, All Around the Town. . . .*

"But I've never stopped missing Warren. He would have loved my success. He'd play golf all day—and leave the writing to me!"

# MARY HIGGINS CLARKE

# For eight years running, he

was NBC's comedic boy wonder, sporting those pinchable cheeks and hysterical one-liners, a teenager ultimately earning $60,000 a week, making him the highest paid child star in history.

Today, six years after actor Gary Coleman bade his final adieu as Arnold Jackson on *Diff'rent Strokes,* he is an unemployed actor sitting on $7 million in assets and a mountain of disappointment.

"The ups have been wonderful," says Coleman, now twenty-four and living on an annual income of $750,000, "but the downs in this business can be horrendous. Eight years playing Arnold, seven TV movies and two theatrical films later, it doesn't seem I'm appreciated. Why? Why? That's a sticky, icky question. I'm not going to get into racism—that TV producers only want the beautiful people—blond, tall, muscular, blue eyes, and white.

"There are many *many* parts I *could* play," says the four-foot-eight-inch actor, the victim of chronic kidney disease.

Having come through two unsuccessful kidney transplants, the actor is surviving with no kidneys and performs dialysis on himself four times daily.

"I'm feeling very energetic," he insists, "and I certainly *could*

work if I wanted to. I believe I can live at least until I'm seventy as long as I do the dialysis and control my hypertension." But, he says, his condition is aggravated by his ongoing lawsuit against his former manager and parents that charges misappropriation of $1 million in funds.

Estranged from his family and unwanted in Hollywood, Coleman, an only child, lives in Denver, a loner who spends most of his time with his pet lizard Pokey, distrustful and disillusioned. "I'm even more distrustful of people than ever before—I've learned to be more protective of myself and my possessions."

That means no romance. "Dating," he says, "doesn't interest me and that doesn't make me gay. I am not afraid to say that I am a virgin. Sexual activity makes relationships turn ugly."

All this adds up to an astonishing announcement: "I am retiring from show business," Coleman exclaims, "because I'm happy, not because I'm too ill to work.

"I am," he also adds, "angry—and bored waiting around six years for people to control my destiny and pull my strings, which infuriates me. I have better things to do.

"I feel unappreciated," Coleman says, "and if I can control my own destiny, a period of my being gone may be good for me. I can be content with what I have and with what I've done.

"I am proud. . . . I'm just sorry that nobody else can be proud."

# GARY COLEMAN

57

# Prim and proper young maidens

of London's exclusive St. Francis school—virgins of the late 1950s who pooh-poohed alcohol, cigarettes and sexual cravings—were mightily titillated by a bad-girl renegade named Jackie.

"At fourteen, I wrote sexy little serials—early *Twin Peaks*—and sold them to kids for a few pennies," says the queen of sex potboilers, Jackie Collins, reigning with her latest Hollywood saga, the novel *Lady Boss.* Its heroine, named Lucky, is a scrapper mined from Collins's own soul.

"Yup," she continues. "I was a rebel, totally wild. I used those pennies, played truant, and took myself to the movies all day. It was," she laughs, "*good* for me. I also smoked. I even waved to the resident flasher."

She also got expelled at fifteen: "Getting thrown out of school was *the* turning point. My male chauvinist father laughed when I told him I wanted to be a writer. He said: 'Goodbye, go to Hollywood and be a movie star like your sister,'" rising starlet Joan, eight years older.

"I was a sharp sixteen, I'd been around, did bit parts, was hit on constantly by married men, and had absolutely no talent for acting."

Then the gloom back in England: "At eighteen, I married a handsome man being treated for severe depression with methedrine—speed. He was crazy—always either up or in a psychiatric hospital. It was very sad. I stayed married four years, but couldn't take it. There I was with a drug addict husband—who died after I divorced him—a young daughter, no money, and a mother dying of cancer. Very tough time. But I *knew* I was going to come through it, *knew* I was going to write."

Rage was the fuel. "I became incensed with the double standard of crude married men who constantly came on to me. Married guys thought they could have a quickie on the road, that their wives were 'different.' Crap. Women can do whatever men can do, and just as well."

Saying so first in her 1960 bestseller, *The World Is Full of Married Men,* Collins then unleashed her steamy prose in *The Stud, Sinners, The Bitch, Hollywood Wives, Hollywood Husbands,* and *Rock Star*. And seeing her through 100 million copies sold in thirty countries is her husband, L.A. disco king Oscar Lerman, who owns the trendy club Tramps.

He "boosted me," she smiles, "*forced* me to finish that first book."

Her success she attributes to "hard work and destiny." And, she concludes, "Telling stories is a gift. When I sit down, the characters take me over. I don't plan it out."

Her motto? "Girls can do anything."

59

# JACKIE COLLINS

# Joan Collins has never had a

picture-perfect love life.

At age seventeen, she says, she was drugged and raped by British actor Maxwell Reed, then, during their marriage, nearly prostituted by him to an Arab sheik for 10,000 pounds.

She says husband number two, Anthony Newley, drove her crazy with his dalliances.

Record producer Ron Kass, now deceased, was a loving husband, but his substance abuse killed their relationship.

But about the fourth go-round, with Swedish smoothie Peter Holm? *"That* marriage was the biggest mistake I've ever made in my life," says Collins, who used her own life experiences researching her last novel, *Love and Desire and Hate.*

"I know something about all three," she jokes over lunch.

How did she make such a mistake? *"Mmmmmm,"* she smiles, munching on asparagus and poached salmon. "I don't know. I was in love. He put the poison in me."

The couple, married in 1985, divorced eighteen months later, and Holm petitioned the courts for $80,000-a-month alimony.

"A little much?" she shrieks, already $2 million poorer thanks to Holm. "I didn't see the oppor-

tunism and deceit until later. Peter viewed me as the money machine. He couldn't have earned that kind of money on his own. Who can?"

Joan could: The *Dynasty* barracuda earned $100,000 per episode.

In all her marriages, the fifty-nine-year-old Joan says, a familiar pattern would emerge: "I never felt my father loved or cared about me enough, and I thought if I could get a difficult man to fall in love with me, I could say to myself: 'I'm a worthwhile person at last. Daddy loves me, and I've got him.'"

No longer looking for approval or for men obsessed with themselves, Joan says she's now suspicious of suitors drawn to her and she has set a few ground rules: "I won't let a man strip my identity and negate my feelings ever again, nor will I be manipulated or exploited by *anyone.*"

Wouldn't Collins be better off with a man of her own generation? "God, no. I like younger men, who don't bring into a relationship ex-wives, pain, and sciatica. A young man is more fresh, enthusiastic, prettier. That may sound shallow, but the physical is important to me."

So what has Collins learned about men?

"Cher said it best. 'You could write everything I know about men on the head of a pin and still have room for the Lord's prayer.'" Amen.

# JOAN COLLINS

61

# Long before he performed

delicate microsurgery at Harvard Medical School, the aggressive boy from Woodside, Queens, had displayed an unusual propensity for anything tactile.

He would patiently erect intricate miniature ships and airplane models, ignoring his schoolwork, and punch his way into the principal's office.

"I was a mild behavior problem with great hand-eye coordination," jokes ophthalmologist-turned-novelist Robin Cook, the reigning king of the so-called techno-medical thriller. His last pulse-quickener was titled *Blindsight.*

"But until the sixth grade," Cook exclaims, "I wasn't even interested in science." A visit to Manhattan's Museum of Natural History changed that, interesting him in archaeology, but when a school chum got injured, his ambitions shifted again.

"He broke his leg in a football game and I had a terrible feeling of helplessness, of incompetence. From then on I wanted the power of a doctor." But while working his way through Columbia Medical School selling vacuum cleaners and cleaning out monkey cages, Cook began to sour on medicine, too.

In 1969, he said, "My forty-fifth gall bladder operation was a

great turning point for me. I had just removed a gall bladder out of an enormously fat woman, held it up, and admitted I wasn't enjoying myself. But across the hall, a colleague was performing eye surgery to classical music, looking through a microscope, doing nice little things with no blood, no bad smells. That did it—I'd become an eye surgeon."

Drafted into the navy during the Vietnam War, Cook doctored by days and moonlighted nights with a typewriter. He churned out his first novel, *The Year of the Intern,* a disillusioning look at the medical profession, in 1973. It didn't sell.

"I was crushed. I started thinking maybe I ought to learn how to write, so I read one hundred bestsellers, over and over, figuring out what made them work."

Attending Harvard Medical School armed with a $10,000 book advance, Cook diligently hammered away at his next novel, *Coma,* a Hitchcockian suspense thriller about supplying transplant organs. Published in paperback in 1977, it sold eleven million copies and was turned into a Hollywood film.

"Luck," he said, "favors the prepared mind." And his mind was delivering precautionary messages about medical care and research.

"Absolutely. 'Buyer beware' turned out to be the recurrent theme in all my books," which includes such best sellers as *Brain, Fever, Mindbend,* and *Vital Signs.*

"Exposing the mess of American medicine is my job," says the author, hammering out his fourteenth novel ensconced in a Naples, Florida, mansion. His medical practice is a distant memory, although he remains an ophthalmologist on permanent leave from the Massachusetts Eye and Ear Infirmary.

"I still consider myself a physician first," he insists, "but I wouldn't be as effective treating a relatively small number of patients privately. Now I think of my patient load in the millions!"

# ROBIN COOK

63

# There is a real Jenny Craig

behind the commercials and the hype.

With husband Sid Craig, she reigns over a unique weight-loss empire consisting of more than six hundred Jenny Craig diet centers that they say yielded $400 million in sales last year—making it the sixth fastest-growing private company in the United States.

The recipe for such success? Set up diet centers everywhere, charge $185 for personalized counseling, and sell fifty-two different frozen meals on the premises.

"We take *away* the need to make decisions about what to eat," says Craig. Bingo.

Not bad for a poor New Orleans girl named Jenny Guidroz, the youngest of six Cajun kids, who first considered becoming a dental hygienist. "But," she recalls, "my mother was a sweetaholic, had three strokes and died when she was forty-nine; I had to take care of her instead of going to college."

Next, marrying a building contractor at age twenty-two, Jenny the housewife was soon modeling, and selling cookware and silver from her home while raising daughter Denise. All was well until 1959.

"That was a real turning point in my life. During my second pregnancy, I had uncontrollable, violent nausea—constant vomiting.

Every twenty minutes I was eating crackers and ginger ale, then peanut butter and jelly, then ice cream, anything."

A blimp after daughter Michelle was born, "I was desperate to lose forty-five extra pounds," says Craig.

Then she planted herself in a New Orleans gym.

"Losing that weight was like watching a metamorphosis. I was astonished by the change in my self-esteem. I started wearing makeup, was fixing my hair again, felt bubbly. I thought if improving the *outside* could make such a profound difference *inside*, this was what I wanted to do."

Managing health clubs in Louisiana for a decade, Jenny shed unwanted pounds and kept them off. She also shed her husband of twenty-two years in 1971.

"The marriage was crumbling. . . . I was always a very self-disciplined person; he wasn't."

New figure, new life. Meanwhile, beginning in 1970, Jenny had started working in Los Angeles for Sid Craig and his Body Contour Inc. Figure Salons.

Almost at once, love blossomed. "We were working together constantly. I told him I was in the process of getting divorced, and he said, 'So am I.' The couple married

in 1979 and started Jenny Craig Inc. in 1983, riding the fitness and diet craze.

"He's a genius at marketing, I'm a more nitty-gritty operational person," says the sixty-year-old millionaire, at five-foot-five a lean 120 pounds, thanks in part to a four-mile run each day.

Does she believe in accident, hard work, or destiny?

"I believe in service—good food and counselors that care—*and* fate. If mother hadn't gotten sick, and if I hadn't been so sick during my pregnancy, I don't know if I'd be here. Making a left-hand turn instead of a right makes all the difference."

# 65

# JENNY CRAIG

# When leggy Tony Curtis camped

it up in drag for *Some Like It Hot*, he was indisputably one of Hollywood's Golden Boys, pulling in big money, sporting three wives, six children (Jamie Lee Curtis included), and headaches to match.

"For me, success and happiness were definitely *not* related," says the actor.

"When I was twelve, my nine-year-old brother was killed by a truck," Curtis shudders. "It was horrible. I had to identify his body. I grew up in poverty in the Bronx, and I was a member of a notorious street gang—dispossessed and kicked out of settlement homes all my life."

By the time Hollywood discovered him in 1949, Curtis faced devastating emotional problems.

"I was filled with pain, despair, nagging doubts, and feelings of not having accomplished anything properly. I had that in common with Marilyn Monroe [his costar in *Some Like It Hot}*.]"

Curtis was powerless over addictions to drugs and alcohol, and his career fizzled to nothing. At the end of the 1970s, he finally sank to rock bottom:

"I was drinking constantly, smoking and free-basing cocaine and prescription drugs, had no fruitful relationship, had alienated my family and friends, didn't like

the way my career was going, my looks were fading too, and I was *broke*.

"I was," he adds, "also filled with *envy*, feeling I deserved parts I wasn't getting. My self-esteem was *lost*."

In desperation, Curtis turned to Alcoholics Anonymous, a revelation: "The program literally allowed me to resurrect my life. I slowly unpeeled the pain of my brother's death. . . .

"Suddenly, I gave up my neurotic-paranoid Hollywood friends, I sold everything I owned and moved from L.A. to Hawaii, and I allowed my attorney to reorganize my financial life."

Finally, Curtis embraced his lifelong passion for painting, recently selling more than one hundred of his acrylic still lifes and celebrity portraits for $1 million.

"Painting gives me tremendous peace. My painting of Marilyn," Curtis tells me in parting, "would please her. I made her neck longer, her waist thinner, her breasts bigger, and her posterior smaller. She'd be alive today if we understood alcoholism as a disease back then. Thank God for the AA program."

# TONY CURTIS

# Will they or won't they? Get

divorced, that is. Married three times each, Vic Damone and Diahann Carroll were recently legally separated, but still, apparently, good friends. When we left off, Diahann Carroll's third husband had just driven himself off a cliff. It was 1977. She vowed never to marry again.

So did Damone, whose first two wives died of drug overdoses, tragedies compounded by his 1970 bankruptcy and compulsive workaholism that wrecked yet a third marriage.

"Grade B movie stuff," quips the crooner, sixty, his voice velvety as ever.

"I never wanted to get married again either when I met Diahann because I really was free," Damone says. His first wife, Pier Angeli, "a lovely, immature girl determined to be an actress," died of a drug overdose.

"My second wife, Judy, had curvature of the spine and got addicted to Valium and Demerol. The same day I declared bankruptcy, she filed for divorce, leaving me with our son and three daughters. Two years later, the poor kids found her dead from an overdose."

Third wife, Becky, twenty years younger, "was not interested in suburban life," says Damone, "and she felt trapped by an older man with kids." That marriage failed in 1982. "I finally learned that a man with babies getting older doesn't need marriage."

But in 1983, Damone and Carroll, longtime but distant acquaintances, accidentally met while staying at the same hotel in San Francisco. Recalls Carroll, "He was very much the ladies' man and I didn't trust him."

"She hated me, really hated me—and I couldn't stand her either," jokes Damone.

A few months later the couple accidentally met again in Palm Beach, booked on the same concert bill.

"It aggravated me that she opened the show," Damone says, "and I tried to stay away from her." Yet after the show, Carroll invited Damone to her room. "I felt attracted to him in a frightening way. I kept it inside but we sat there talking all night and had our first kiss."

After a two-and-a-half-year courtship, Carroll was itchy for the license: "I wanted to know where we were going, and that was it."

Damone: "I was scared and I'm still scared. Our attorney told us we should sign a prenuptial, but we wouldn't, and didn't feel we were making a mistake." Alas, the marriage has, at times, collapsed, only to be jump-started once again.

"Our marriage has been difficult to keep and make lasting because of her independence and mine," says Damone, who loves to cook Italian food almost as much as he loves to sing. "I got angry at her before our separation because we set the budget for redecorating our kitchen at $50,000 and it cost $174,000!"

Carroll: "It's a beautiful kitchen."

Now we'll see who gets to cook in it!

# VIC DAMONE

# Phyllis Diller struts out to nightclub

audiences done up in her pink, yellow and orange Dynel gown and outrageous wig, aflight with Barbara Bush swimsuit calendar and Dan Quayle blooper jokes. Still, lampooning herself remains her forte.

The seventy-five-year-old comedian doesn't hesitate to talk about her 350 blonde wigs and eleven plastic surgeries. On stage, however, she never discusses the key to remaining energetic and positive.

But to me she declares, "I'm *never* in a bad mood—I don't allow it."

She was, however, once upon a time, a woman surrounded by a complaining husband and a coterie of negative friends who depressed her.

"My father called them crepehangers . . . voices of doom, and he avoided them like the plague. I wasn't so lucky. I was saturated by a group of ten crepehangers—plus a husband." But in 1975, Diller divorced her second hubby (Ward Anderson Donovan), a refreshment that set into motion a change of life at age fifty-eight.

"He was a belligerent and unreasonable drunk with a hot temper and a mean mouth. I finally decided *not to put up with anybody*

*negative in my life.* I wanted them O-U-T—and I started with him."

Next in line were nine so-called friends. Why?

"They would tell me their troubles," Diller explains. "My listening didn't help—it only hindered and enabled the problems to grow and become ugly monsters. One woman complained about her marriage, though she didn't have the guts to leave it.

"Another on my list was always late.

"Another I *know* wouldn't give me the time of day if I weren't famous. He's a starsucker.

"Another woman was a motormouth. She'd ambush me, and not know how to say goodbye. These are women who have nothing to do—empty shells. Their children are gone, marriages dead, they've never worked, and there's no hope for them."

Diller also eliminated her wardrobe designer of seventeen years—"a motormouth and a complainer who literally wanted to *be* me." And so on.

And so: "My secretaries now have by the phones a neatly typed list of people. To 'The Nine' I am permanently out of town. Would you believe one woman still calls after ten years? She wants to fix me up on dinner dates.

"Don't lie down with dogs," Diller advises. "You'll march around with fleas. The key to happiness is surrounding yourself with positive thinkers."

# PHYLLIS DILLER

71

# Ever since Issur Danielovitch

changed his name to Kirk Douglas and claimed instant stardom as a prizefighter in *Champion* in 1949, the square-jawed actor with the dimpled chin has never looked back. He survived Roman legions, rival gunslingers, and a sliced ear in some of his seventy-nine Hollywood films—and even pulled through a midair helicopter collision in February 1991 with mere cuts and bruises.

"That was sheer luck and life is awfully sweet," grins the screen icon, who claims that a true turning point in recent years has been his unexpected change of profession.

"After forty-two years on screen, I never intended to become a writer, but I did anyway." It all started with his best-selling 1988 autobiography, *The Ragman's Son.*

Next, thanks to super-agent Irving (Swifty) Lazar, he signed a two-book, $2 million deal with Random House that yielded his first novel, the well-received *Dance With the Devil.*

"I can see in retrospect that this career was coming," Douglas explains. "For my entire life, I've been intrigued with what people do to survive. I had reached a point in my life when I wanted *to stop*—to take inventory and find out where I came from, and where I was going.

"So about ten years ago, I began scribbling down ideas for *Dance With the Devil,* intrigued by the story of a man who'd been in a concentration camp and later lived his entire life as a lie, claiming not to be a Jew. That lie becomes a burden. It suddenly hit me. I ought to tell the story of my *own* life, so I put the novel aside and wrote *Ragman* as a kind of catharsis, and later went back to *Devil.*

"I wrote *Ragman,*" he continues "with my gut, my instincts— nothing formal. Writing is meditative and I like the solitude.

"When I started adding up the pluses and minuses of my life, I found I began to *like* myself.

"I learned that maturity is getting to know yourself, it's digging deep into your guts. Most people go through life kidding themselves, never getting to that point of looking into the mirror. That took a long time for me to do." Having done so, he says, "I discovered that in a novel I could actually dig and say *more* about myself than in autobiography.

"I won't give you an example," he adds, laughing.

"I still don't feel very secure as a writer," the star continues. "One robin doesn't make a spring. But after you've made almost eighty movies, you think: 'Gee,

maybe the people have seen enough of me.' *I've* seen enough of me! So I've learned that writing is an extension of acting. Now I play all the roles: I decide who has sex, who doesn't. I'm expressing myself and take all the credit or all the blame."

# KIRK DOUGLAS

# In the dog days of the

Depression, a penniless eighteen-year-old farmboy from Lima, Ohio, bemoaned the fact that upon graduation from high school, he couldn't afford a class ring.

Nor had he ever been able to soar down a country hill on his own, shiny new bike.

"I was the poorest kid in my class," recalls Hugh Downs of *20/20*, now celebrating more than fifty years in broadcasting and, at seventy, just back from a Florida deep dive onto artificial reefs.

"I used to search junkyards for bicycle parts," he says. "My father eventually bought me a secondhand bike," but the scar of deprivation remained.

It was in early May 1939, after his one-year scholarship to Bluffton (Ohio) College expired, that Downs's father, a Westinghouse factory worker, ordered his son to get a job.

"There I was, coming home from a little grocery store, carrying a discounted gallon jug of milk, and I happened to come upon our local radio station," the super-low budget WLOK, which pumped out a measly hundred watts.

"Desperate for any job, I asked what it took to be a radio announcer, and the receptionist told me auditions were on Friday. It was Tuesday.

"So I picked up my milk jug and started to leave.

"But, suddenly, from out of nowhere, an eavesdropping program director said: 'I can listen to you right now.'"

"I put my milk jug back down, read some commercial copy for a paint-store ad and was told, 'That was very bad . . . *really terrible,*' but great oaks from little acorns grow."

"I was hired," Downs beams, "for a princely $12.50 per seven-day week."

From there, things improved for Downs with *Kukla, Fran & Ollie,* to sidekicking for Jack Paar on *The Tonight Show*, to hosting *Concentration*, then *Today*, then, since 1978, coanchoring *20/20* with Barbara Walters. "But just before buying that jug of milk," Downs recounts, "I had almost been hired by a roofing company. And five years earlier, I was determined to be a portrait painter—I was quite a remarkable draftsman even as a child—but I discovered I was color-blind and dropped that idea.

"And so," he laughs, "if I hadn't been color-blind, if the roofing company had hired me, I'd probably be sitting on a roof, painting! Radio was my second choice.

"I bought that milk and turned down that road.

"But what if I had gone down a different street?"

# HUGH DOWNS

75

# In tiny Townsend, Montana

(pop. 600), a teenager named Patrick—the son of a couple of just-getting-by bartenders, Terrence and Marie Duffy—was Joe Average, and nothing more.

"I was an average student—all C's," laughs Patrick Duffy, "and average at track and football." But the six-foot-two jock found his niche at the University of Washington as an actor, only to lose it in his senior year.

"I overextended myself by fiendishly rehearsing and performing," Duffy remembers, "then I got a bad case of laryngitis and went into the gym and screamed and yelled until my voice came back. A month later, I started hemorrhaging until the blood vessels in my vocal cords finally ruptured."

The prognosis was grim: "The specialist said I'd never act again, period, though I could probably speak normally if I followed a regimen of total vocal rest."

Depressed but compliant, the twenty-one-year-old consoled himself by taking classes in marionette-making and pantomime until he hit romantic and medical paydirt in 1972, the year a New York-based dance company landed in town with a ballerina named Carlyn Rosser in tow.

"You can get as Shirley MacLaine-ish as you want at this part in the story," offers Duffy, "but Carlyn converted me." From? To? "From lethargy to the orthodox Nichiren Shoshi sect of Buddhism. She told me the problem with my voice was my own making, that I could change my karma by chanting. At first I was skeptical, but she said she'd be there morning and evening to help me learn.

"Chanting the words *Nam-myohorenge-kyo* [meaning "Hail to the Lotus Sutra," the Sutra being the collection of Buddhist writings of the thirteenth-century "good" or "true" law] should have been medically disastrous, but my voice grew in strength beyond what the doctor could believe. Three months after meeting Carlyn, I was acting again!"

After eighteen years of "a happy marriage" to Carlyn, and his twenty-one years of chanting (sons Padraic and Conor join in, too), Duffy says his spiritual life has been "renovated."

"I started chanting with a list of things I wanted for myself," says Duffy, "but for the past eighteen years, ninety-nine percent of the time I spend chanting for other people. I've learned that my main job as a human being is trying to make other people happy.

"Buddhism has been the bottom line" to his success, says Duffy, plus an athlete's appetite for victory over the odds of a poor upbringing, a broken voice, show-biz dog days before *Dallas*, and the tragedy of both parents being shot dead at their Montana tavern in 1986.

"If you don't want something bad enough to never give up, then you have to accept failure if it presents itself; but if you never give up, then you will never fail. I don't have my ear to the great tuba of life, but I've learned to accept all obstacles as dangerous opportunities and continue on."

# PATRICK DUFFY

# The spunky Irish-Cherokee girl

from Henderson, Texas, drilled away at her dream, knocking out ballet-tap-jazz-and-acrobat moves until she dropped. Finally, her spiky incandescence landed her the starring role in *Funny Face*, a highly touted situation comedy that aired in 1971. Thus, at age twenty-five, Sandy Duncan's dream had finally come true.

"But the dream was actually the beginning of a horrible *nightmare*," counters Duncan, describing tragic events that stole from her the first blush of success.

"All I remember from 1971 was an excruciating headache that never stopped, blinding pain. I could just barely keep my eyes open."

"For weeks," Duncan remembers, "my vision had gotten worse and worse in my left eye—it felt like Vaseline covering it—and two months into filming I was *totally* blind in that eye. Doctors were giving me massive doses of cortisone and diagnosing the loss of vision as optic neuritis, i.e., stress. I started to think I was going *nuts, losing it.* They're telling me it's all in my head?"

Duncan finally dumped UCLA Hospital specialists for her hometown doctor in Tyler, Texas. "He said: 'Oh, hell, you don't have

no optic neuritis, you got something pressin' on the optic nerve.'"

Sure enough, a fibroid tumor the size of a walnut had lodged behind her left eye. "I got myself a good neurosurgeon, he took the top of my head off and removed the tumor."

Duncan permanently lost the vision in her left eye. *Funny Face* vanished, and the revamped *Sandy Duncan Show* flopped the next season.

"Producers were saying I was finished, but I have real strong survival instincts. It was denial, though I never experienced self-pity. At first, I had a lot of self-consciousness, felt very insecure about my eye straying and had to have muscle correction surgery. Then I had to adjust to losing my depth perception. False eyelashes were out of the question. I'd glue them on my cheeks."

Through it all, Duncan kept her spirits up. "Losing my vision, I realize, was a gift. Yes, it was. I don't even *think* about its being bad luck. It was a good turning point because I was not ready for success. I was being manipulated as a bubbly creature constantly up. It took me years to grow out of that. The tumor delivered me from buying my own act. I also wouldn't be as brave if it hadn't happened."

Starring recently in a twenty-six exercise warmup titled *The 5 Minute Workout*, Duncan displays a conditioned body and an exuberant aura. Does that signal total acceptance of her loss?

"Ahhhh. *Never.* That sense of loss never goes away. I deal with it daily. I *still* live in fear that I may have to face not having any vision because I have one eye and it's nearsighted.

"My kids [Jeffrey and Mike] always tell me to get a handicapped sticker for the car, so we can park up close. But I'm not handicapped. Not at all. I'm lucky!"

# ЅANDY DUNCAN

# U.S. Army Captain Jose Manuel

Fajardo, once an Olympic volleyball bronze medalist, returned home from Vietnam in 1968 a broken man. Crumpled in bed for twelve excruciating years, he suffered from a degenerative neurological disease attributed to Agent Orange. And nursing him, from ages eleven to sixteen, was his little "Glorita."

"Deep down inside, I always had a premonition that I would encounter a disaster, just like Dad," exclaims Latin pop superstar Gloria Estefan, who hovered over her Cuban-refugee father and younger sister Becky, while her mother, Gloria, struggled to eke out a living as a schoolteacher in Miami.

"Dad would lie in bed with his eyes rotating, and eventually lost his mental ability, and I had to wash him and feed him. Very scary and depressing for a teenager." She sometimes fled in tears to her room: "Singing was the only bright spot in my life," she says.

Graduating from the University of Miami in 1979, Estefan had a year earlier married her first boyfriend, accordion player Emilio Estefan, "who motivated me, talking me into singing and songwriting." Estefan sparkled as the vocalist in hubby's band, the Miami Sound Machine.

What began as "just a week-end thing," she says, turned to gold in 1985 with the monster hit, "Conga." Ten million records were sold as sultry Estefan sold out stadiums. Then on March 20, 1990, her tour bus crashed in a snowstorm on I-80, near Tobyhanna, Pennsylvania. "Here it was, *the nightmare* I knew I would somehow encounter," says Estefan, asleep when a speeding semi crashed into the bus from behind: "I felt an explosion, I woke up on the floor with a metallic taste in my mouth, couldn't move my legs, was petrified of being paralyzed. The pain was gruesome and I clung to the hand of my son [Nayib, then seven]. "He broke his collarbone, Emilio broke two ribs," and Estefan broke her back.

"Two vertebrae, T12 and L1," she explains, "were pushed in and separated from the spine, shattered with pieces of bone all over. One more millimeter would have severed the cord and I'd be dead or paralyzed."

Doctors had to slice Estefan's back muscles and insert two eight-inch stainless steel rods to repair the spine. Horrible pain. "For two months, even with morphine, I couldn't sleep longer than forty-five minutes at a time, but my early life prepared me for something like this."

Petrified of becoming a burden to those she loved—"I most definitely did not want to wind up like my father"—Estefan tackled her fate with extensive physical and musical therapy.

"Emilio coaxed me back into writing music though I was afraid," and just ten months later Estefan released a new album, *Into the Light:* "Coming out of the dark," she sings, "I finally see the light. . . . Coming out of the dark, I know the love that saved me. . . .

Since her triumphant return to the stage on March 1, 1991, the singer has danced her way to total recovery: "I've done over ninety-five shows since that first show, run six and a half miles every other day, plus weight training, and the stair-master. I wanted to prove you can deal with a problem and get beyond it."

# GLORIA ESTEFAN

# Never turn down a party

invitation. "I didn't," laughs Mia Farrow, remembering New Year's Eve 1980.

"That was the year Woody invited me to his annual holiday party," she recalls, and shortly thereafter her collaboration with Woody Allen—professional and romantic—began. Among other benefits, it provided Farrow a revitalized film career and a father for her brood, now numbering eleven.

When Farrow met the offbeat director, "It wasn't love at first sight, but a few weeks later we started seeing each other regularly—the rest just happened." Allen became instant dad, big-time: There are Farrow's twins by André Previn, Matthew and Sacha; Fletcher, also a Previn; the adopted Vietnamese girls, Soon-Yi and Lark; and the Korean children, Daisy and Moses. Adding to the group, Allen (with Farrow) adopted Dylan, and took the biological plunge himself in 1988 by fathering his first child, Satchel. "Knock on wood," Farrow laughs. "Woody turned out to be a gentle, supportive pal to all the kids and for me—the perfect remedy. He definitely changed my life."

She had had two unhappy marriages, a disastrous one to Frank Sinatra in 1966 and a healthier one to conductor Previn in 1970. "But

neither marriage worked," Mia deadpans. Indeed, Sinatra bitterly opposed Farrow's ambition to continue acting, and she once turned up on a set with welts all over her body. "He wanted a woman who would just stay at home."

So did Previn. "André was always gone," she remembers. "He hated the movies and didn't want me in bad ones—though those were the only kind I could make so close to home."

Allen, on the other hand, does nothing but cook up made-to-order roles for Farrow, thus far, his love for her unfettered by the legalities of marriage. "Woody is secure enough not to need that legal piece of paper," says Farrow, who recently adopted two more children. "We're *one* family but we don't live together. It would be too disruptive because we both need time alone. I like the idea of seeing one another in our prime time—when we want to.

"All my life, it seems I lived with a man and it was always *his* house. Now, if I want to hang a picture, I hang it. It's *my* house."

# MIA FARROW

# Don't let Farrah Fawcett's

breathy, buttery voice fool you. She can be a hard rock, like the wedding diamond she'll never wear, "because marriage," she tells me, "is purely a business contract. It kills romance."

No problem there: Even after twelve years, after she and Ryan O'Neal make love, she confides, sometimes "he reaches over to me and he'll say: 'I'm not kidding you, you've got to marry me.'"

Nothing doing. Farrah is permanently soured on even the whiff of male domination, and to understand just why, let us turn to . . .

"*The* point," she laughs, back in 1977, when she divorced her husband, fired her manager, and quit *Charlie's Angels.*

He-hunk Lee Majors first discovered the Texas beauty two weeks after she arrived in Hollywood to model. But their five-year marriage left her cold: "Men are funny," Farrah muses. "They're attracted to independent, strong women, and the thing that irritates and threatens them most is that independence."

Unlike O'Neal, an emotional chatterbox who doesn't hesitate to pick a verbal fight, "Lee was silent. I much prefer Ryan. Lee didn't talk. He thought I *should* come home and make the dinner. And he didn't

support my leaving the show," a reference to Farrah's controversial exit from *Charlie's Angels* after only one season, due to her resentment over the show's egregious T&A sensibilities.

"The male producers kept patting me on the head," says the woman who was blackballed for five years in Hollywood after leaving, "while I was complaining that the characters had no depth. They had none."

That same year, Fawcett also fired her manager, Hollywood publicist Jay Bernstein, who had discovered her and made her a $100,000-a-year model: "Again, there was a man who needed too much control over me and he kept taking credit for everything I had done. His ego needed that.

"First I spent time not hurting his feelings, but finally I wanted to slap his face and say: 'Excuse me! You didn't make me. Everybody has an ego and eccentricities and I have enough of my own without somebody else's coming into play. You're fired, get out.'"

Now don't go messing with the tough, sexy, driven star of TV films like *Extremities* and *The Burning Bed*, or you, too, will get your fingers singed.

"I'm my own woman," she finishes, "and Ryan likes me that way. He's never said, 'Don't do it.'"
He better not.

# FARRAH FAWCETT

# Setting out one sun-drenched

day from his Trinchera Ranch, at Fort Garland, Colorado, the late Malcolm Forbes climbed aboard his black and red Harley Davidson FLHS, eager for a twelve-hour run over Glacier National Park's Going to the Sun Highway.

Flying over winding roads and hidden crevices toward western Montana, the then-sixty-four-year-old Forbes rounded a bend onto a gravel patch, and, Forbes said, "In only one second my bike flew away from me."

The Harley crashed crazily due west, Forbes's leather-clad crumpled body was thrown east, and he was rescued by a helicopter medical unit that patched together three broken ribs and a collapsed lung.

"But," the indefatigable mogul beamed in an interview a month before his death, "it was nine days later, a beautiful day in New Jersey and I was feeling better." So abrasions and all, up he went in a golden balloon christened Sphinx II, flown over Egypt on a Forbes friendship salute in 1984.

"We climbed faster than we should have, to three thousand feet, and the top deflation panel literally exploded, blew its top. We went straight down like a rock and I said: 'Dammit, why now? Why now? I'll

be dead in a minute . . . knocking on the pearly gates. . . .'"

But instead, missing a steel power box by two feet, he crashed into a mudpile. "When we hit, I thought I'd be dead. But I lucked out two times in a row."

Climbing out into the muck, hardly heaven, Forbes had his revelation: "I suddenly thought, 'Time is the single most precious limited commodity we have.' *There is a limit to time* . . . you can't assume perpetuity. I suddenly became more conscious of my good luck and realized it was quite extraordinary to be able to throw my leg out of bed in the morning."

He biked and ballooned until his death at age seventy in February 1990. Forbes said: "Death will be the final exciting experience, though I'm not eager for it. If a cat has nine lives, I'm up to ten."

And he was still throwing caution to the wind: "My God, yes," exclaimed Forbes, whose last-published work was *More Than I Dreamed*, an illustrated catalogue of his motorcycles, balloons, yachts, and planes, with matching anecdotes. "You can't go through life insulating yourself from danger. *Everything* is dangerous. Living is dangerous. Eventually, everybody dies of it. I keep moving.

"And," he said in parting, "I don't waste time. If there's something that turns me on I do it now. This life isn't a dry run."

# MALCOLM FORBES

# She was a precocious

five-year-old from Great Neck, Long Island—an expert at crafting paper dolls and a whiz at reading the *World-Telegram* with her businessman dad, Nathaniel. But that day, she was staring into the mirror, entranced with herself.

Having pinched her mother Loretta's best chiffon morning gown, red satin heels, and a parasol, little Eileen Ford then traipsed out onto the driveway to show off her outfit.

"Unfortunately, I got stuck in a tar pit, and mother wasn't very pleased," laughs modeling mogul Ford, grande dame of Ford Models Inc., the international agency with billings of $42 million per year. She runs it with husband and cofounder, Jerry Ford.

Just back from China in search of "the supermodel of the world," the peripatetic seventy-year-old claims to harness as much energy today as she did forty-five years ago, when her upper-crust mother predicted she'd become a lawyer.

"But that was not to be," says Ford. A Barnard grad, she was fascinated with fashion and first worked as a stylist-copywriter and photographer's assistant. "Still, I wasn't sure what I was going to do until I met Jerry Ford. He was the turning point of my life."

One day, the twenty-two-year-old Eileen was coaxed inside a college hangout, the Gold Rail Bar at 110th Street and Broadway. "At the back of the bar, there stood Jerry Ford, a Navy midshipman. Jerry was nineteen and the *living end*—so good-looking. It took me three weeks of plotting to meet him at a Columbia dance."

The couple married just three months later, in November 1944. What did her mother say? "Not very loving things. Jerry wasn't from a wealthy family, he hadn't finished college, he didn't have a job, and I didn't know him very well." No matter. "I just knew he was right for me."

A month later, Jerry Ford joined his ship in the Pacific, and in 1946, after he returned, Eileen became pregnant. "One model I knew didn't have an agency, and another was with an agency that never paid her. So I said I would take their bookings at home. After the baby was born, I told myself I'd go to law school, but by then I had eight models. Jerry had a football scholarship offer from Notre Dame, but we couldn't afford to move, so we decided to start up a model agency."

That first year, the couple racked up $250,000 in bookings using twenty-two models. Business

only got better, but after ten years, their marriage became strained.

"That was the second turning point. Jerry told me I was too damn bossy, and if I wanted to stay married, I'd have to recognize him as boss. So I said: 'Okay, you're boss.' Now he runs the whole place, and I don't care. Would I rather have my husband or listen to garbage about sexism?"

Ever since, the Ford partnership has flourished, with talents such as Christie Brinkley, Kim Basinger, Jerry Hall, Brooke Shields, and Lauren Hutton, plus a second generation of Fords—Jamie, Bill, Katie, and Lacey.

"I've been the luckiest girl in town," says Ford. "If I hadn't gone into that bar, I would have gone to law school, and I'd be a judge about to retire."

# EILEEN FORD

# That vicious Oakdale woman

known simply as Lisa, suffering and scheming for more than thirty years on *As the World Turns*, is tougher than elephant skin and seasoned to a crisp.

"She's been married six times," giggles soap star Eileen Fulton of her heroine. "She's had thirty-eight lovers, two children, plus one *phantom fetus*." Her wild escapades have filled the public's unquenchable afternoon appetite for soap operas.

"Why not?" Fulton challenges. "What got the public hooked on Shakespeare? Murder, love affairs, and insanity—all real-life situations."

Not to be outdone, in real life Fulton has weathered her own share of heartache over the past thirty years, a soapy love life crammed with three rocky marriages and abuse from her men.

A Methodist preacher's daughter from Asheville, North Carolina, Fulton was petrified of husband number one even before the 1955 marriage: "One day, after fighting about the wedding silver and china, he beat the hell out of an iron picket fence with an umbrella. I should have known. He hit me many times. Six months *after* the wedding, I found some porno pictures in his file cabinet; same day he threw a sandwich in my face. I

finally picked up a pot and cracked him in the head with it—dented the Revereware copper bottom—and told him I wished he was dead." The marriage lasted eighteen months.

Husband number two, circa 1971—"the real love of my life"—hung in for nine years: "We had music and wine for four years—perfection—then it went sour. Total communication breakdown. One day he threatened to kill my brother, and a marriage counselor told me: *Get out fast!* I took my jewelry, credit cards, hot water bottle, and dog, Amelia Earhart, and flew!"

Husband number three, circa 1989, was an impulsive affair: "Met him at a ball, heavy datin' for three months. I popped the question myself, then divorced him three months later. I have evening dresses older." Why the quick split? "I thought he was low-key and calm, but he had a hot temper."

"I told him our divorce was my birthday present to myself."

Alas, the lesson: "Don't be hasty," says the actress, lithe at fifty-nine. "The hot flashes are just wonderful because the cute guys at the cold studio just love to get close to a radiating stove. . . ."

Any regrets? "None. I'm glad it's all out of my system," she concludes, cuddling Pekineses Sarah

Bernhardt and Laurence Olivier, and Shih Tzu Simone Signoret.

"I've had enough. I'm no longer afraid of men—still love them—but I'll never be abused again. Now I talk to myself and I'm not lonely. I got married to share and might do it again. In the meantime, I share with my dogs. They're limited in speech, but not in loyalty."

# EILEEN FULTON

# "Marriage," Eva Gabor once

mused, "is too interesting an experiment to be tried once or twice." So the Hungarian-born beauty walked down the aisle five times (outdone, by the way, by sister Zsa Zsa, who has taken the vows nine times).

"My choices were ghastly, ridiculous," Gabor admits, speaking of her first four husbands—a doctor, a real estate salesman, a surgeon, and an executive. But the fifth marriage was a disaster that nearly destroyed her, she recounts.

"I was married for ten years and under the *impression* that it was very happy," says the Hungarian-born actress of her time with aeronautics tycoon Frank Jameson, whom she wed in 1973. "Then, one night in Paris, I found out that he had a little girlfriend secretary, and literally overnight he destroyed my life!"

And not just emotionally: "I was always independent," says the actress, "always earned a great deal of money," largely from the long-running TV comedy *Green Acres*, still seen daily in fifty-two countries. "But for ten years, believing that a man is the king, I had let my husband manage everything."

Investments? "God only knows," she says, grimacing. "I trusted him." After the divorce, what was left? "Nothing. I still had my jewelry."

Gabor divorced Jameson, then collapsed. "I was broke, in the depths of despair, crying in my office, desolate, completely and utterly destroyed. I cannot tell you the misery. I weighed ninety pounds. I knew I had two choices: Either waste away and die or pull myself together by the roots and start all over again.

"The turning point was therapy. The number one thing I learned is *don't blame yourself*. When a marriage crumbles, blaming is the one thing a woman or a man will do. It's a lot of bunk. I was the best wife to him, the most decent."

Lesson number two? "Through a lot of suffering and thinking, I learned my best friend had to be me. Not a man."

Does that mean losing her fifth husband was some kind of gift? "To be pained and hurt is not a gift. But the beauty is you can come *out* of it."

Within two years, Eva Gabor was furiously acting and promoting Eva Gabor International, the world's largest wig company: "Once I found myself, I learned I had *a very good brain*.

"I didn't need to ask anybody for advice. I decided I was going to make it, bigger than I ever did— and I have. For the first time, I have

a steady income for the rest of my life."

For now, Gabor is glowing and wrinkle-free, summering in the south of France with constant companion Merv Griffin.

Believing there is "nothing uglier than a bitter woman," Gabor says she'd marry again. "Absolutely, I was and am an eternal romantic and always married for love, not money."

What about Griffin? "No, no, I'm not going to marry him. We're best friends and lucky to have each other. But after nine years being unmarried, I like living alone!"

# EVA GABOR

# Sultry even in a maternity

gown, the former Hungarian actress Jolie Gabor and her jeweler husband, Vilmos, sat appalled in a Budapest hospital room. Unlike the couple's gorgeous first-born daughter Magda, or the adorable Eva who would follow, tiny Sari Gabor, two months premature, was a sorry sight indeed.

"I came out *green*," laughs the irrepressible Zsa Zsa Gabor, "and very ugly," an infant destined to race through a dizzying array of fifty-six films, nine marital escapades, seventeen racehorses, eight dogs and an array of amorous run-ins with the likes of Sean Connery, Charlie Chaplin, Frank Sinatra, and Richard Burton.

"I'm the most impulsive person," booms the Princess, married in 1986 to her ninth husband—"my last"—Prince Fredrich von Anhalt, Duke of Saxony. "I've collected," she explains, "frogs all my life, decorative ones and husbands, but it took all this time to find myself a Prince!"

Desperate to escape politically unstable Hungary, Gabor, a teenager, first married a forty-five-year-old Turkish government official, Burhan Belge, in 1937. "He took me to Turkey but never had sex with me," she laughs. But then she met the Turkish ruler, Mustata

Kemal Ataturk: "I lost my virginity to a god."

Next came husband No. 2, in 1942, Conrad Hilton, another oldie at sixty-one: "I liked gray-haired men, but I never married for money. Conrad treated me terribly, was unfaithful to me with fifteen-year-old girls. I walked away with a six-week-old baby," daughter Francesca.

In 1949, she married actor George Sanders, who was equally unfaithful, "mentally torturing me," she says, forcing her into a retaliatory affair with Latin stud Porfiro Rubirosa: "Ruby was the best lover in bed. No equal. He was like a drug."

Following a ten-year respite from marriage, Gabor married businessman Herbert Hutner in 1964—"the dearest man . . . it ended because he was too good for me. I need a shit." Next, Texan oil magnate Joshua Cosden, in 1966: "An arriviste! Looked like Jimmy Stewart, but an impossible racist. Called Sammy Davis Jr. a darkie and couldn't stand my Jewish friends."

Then came Barbie Doll inventor Jack Ryan, in 1975. She later found out about his female mistresses, homosexual affairs, and sexual torture chamber: "He just killed himself recently, shot himself in the head. When I found out

about his secret life, I divorced him," marrying her divorce lawyer, Michael O'Hara, in 1977: "He was gorgeous, but a Yugoslav and a Hungarian don't mix."

Mexican businessman Felipe Alba, circa 1982, she claims she never married at all: "He tried to marry me but it never happened. He wanted my name and my money."

So many husbands: "Don't count them! When the butler in England brings my breakfast, the man in bed has to be my husband." Promiscuous? "Absolutely not. My best friend Grace Kelly slept with more men in a month than I was married to."

What has she learned? "Nothing. If you live like I do, enjoying every moment, you never give up years in misery or complaining.

"Darling"—she smiles in parting—"you have *one* life to live. What the hell. Why would anyone want to sit home and brood?"

# ZSA ZSA GABOR

# Fifty years ago, Mervyn Edward

Griffin was a sixteen-year-old kid in San Mateo, California, with a golden voice—a 240-pound blimp who charged $15 to sing at weddings, $20 for funerals.

"I could also play the piano like a son of a gun," laughs Griffin, who says he stumbled into the big time thanks to two "oddball" turns in the road.

The first came in 1945. "I auditioned at KFRC radio in San Francisco with a drummer friend, Cal Tjader," Griffin remembers. "I wanted a job playing piano, but they told me they needed singers.

"Cal said: 'Oh, Merv can sing,' so they put a microphone in front of me and I sang 'Sleigh Ride in July.' 'It's good,' the manager told me; the next day, a Friday, I sang on air with an orchestra. I was gutsy, but knew nothing. Afterward, the manager said: 'Monday starts *The Merv Griffin Show*. Period.' I thought this man had really flipped."

He hadn't. Over the next three years, young Griffin churned out eleven shows weekly and raked in $4,400 each month.

Next he toured with Freddy Martin's Orchestra and his trademark song, "I've Got a Lovely Bunch of Coconuts," sold a million copies.

But Merv wasn't satisfied: "I had fame in the record industry, sang for the next seventeen long years, but I wanted more." He got it, winning the host's job on NBC-TV's *Play Your Hunch*.

"Now," Griffin says, "for the second turning point," in 1962: "*Play Your Hunch* came live at 10:30 a.m. from studio 6B, the same studio Jack Paar used for *The Tonight Show*.

"One day, at the point in the show when I said, 'Think it over', the curtain opened and out walked Jack by mistake—he'd come to work early after a dentist appointment.

"The audience started screaming, Jack looked astonished, I grabbed the microphone and said: 'What are you doing here?' Jack, who never gave interviews, said: 'What are *you* doing here? It's *my* studio.' Jack then went up to his office and told his producer: 'That kid is funny; on my next night off, give him the show.' After that, I just went on and on."

On and on included twenty-three years hosting seven thousand episodes of *The Merv Griffin Show* (1964-87), Griffin Enterprises' hugely profitable *Jeopardy* and *Wheel of Fortune*, plus Merv's hotel empire—Resorts in Atlantic City,

Paradise Island in the Bahamas, and the Beverly Hilton Hotel.

"There are no shortcuts to the top," says Griffin. If you plan a career in show business, it never works. Everything that happened to me happened by mistake. I don't believe in fate. It's luck, timing, and accident. Jack Paar walked through the curtain, and my career was made. I think I was born lucky."

# MERV GRIFFIN

# The model-handsome boy savored

a childhood sea-island fantasy— toasting himself on the pristine beaches of Santa Catalina Island, diving for coins underneath the glass-bottomed boat piloted by his father, Cap'n Eddie, and riding the waves of the Pacific on a surfboard. From the outside, everything looked perfect.

"No traffic, no crime, no smog—idyllic," smiles actor Gregory Harrison, who nonetheless faced unending abuse in his early days: "I was raised with the miscon-ception that I *should* be perfect— that anything shy of perfection was failure. Three A's were no excuse for a B." Although he eventually snared the part of Dr. "Gonzo" Gates on *Trapper John, M.D.*, the hit TV series that ran from 1979 to 1986, the perfection-prone actor was slowly and secretly sinking into drug and alcohol addiction: "Trying to be perfect was a heavy weight," he groans, "and I didn't feel any self-esteem, just gnawing discontent," misery numbed by $750,000 worth of cocaine: "Coke made me feel perfect—more cre-ative, intelligent, handsome, witty."

By 1987, after eight years of sniffing and drinking, Harrison was bottoming, his anemic body cov-ered with sores, his 1981 marriage to wife Randi Oakes in tatters, and Hollywood producers wary of him.

"I was willing to do *anything* to hide my strange behavior," he whispers, tears filling his eyes. "For months, it was just me and my con-nection. I became an incessant and incredibly determined liar, paranoid and unpredictable. Even my daugh-ter, Emma, then just one, didn't want to sit in my lap. I looked in the mirror one day and saw death as the only option left to me."

Until the summer of 1987, when Harrison, working on a TV film titled *Hot Paint*, met an actor "who ran his own little AA meeting every day at lunch. I was shocked he could talk with so much self-esteem about his disease while I was so ashamed. The revelation was that *maybe* there was a solution."

In August, Harrison drove himself to the Betty Ford Clinic in Rancho Mirage, California: "From the moment I walked in and quit using, I threw myself into my recovery with the same commit-ment I had thrown myself into self-abuse. Nobody wanted to be sober and free of this terrible life more than me."

Five leap-of-faith years later, life is sweet for Harrison—weight-lifting daily, twelve-stepping other addicts, building a new home in the Northwest, developing a sitcom for CBS through his own Catalina Productions, and acting as national

spokesperson for the substance abuse assistance program called EIRAC (Entertainment Industry Referral and Assistance Center).

"After five years of recovery, every morning I look in the mirror and remind myself that I'm a man with a lifetime disease—only one drink or one snort away from hell."

# GREGORY HARRISON

# There it sat. Silent, vicious,

malignantly festering in the heart of prosperous Weston, Connecticut. Twelve rooms on five acres. The House of Death, The House of Doom.

"That's *exactly* what it was— no exaggeration," exclaims actress Mariette Hartley, who last year described her ordeal in her autobiography, *Breaking the Silence*, the sad, sometimes hilarious saga of a girl raised by suicidally depressed, alcoholic parents.

"Both Mom and Dad were blackout, killer drinkers," Hartley remembers. "Dad came to school football games drunk. I'd find Mom passed out in the bushes, scared and hiding.

"*Her* mother had been terrorized by her own father, a behavioral psychologist who believed that children should be raised without physical affection, to foster their independence.

"I felt unfillable, unlovable. Then, in my teens, I was emotionally 'incested' by Mama. She'd get drunk, then tell me about how terrific Dad was in bed, how she distrusted and hated him. I became the mother, she the daughter. It was devastating."

At age fourteen, Hartley, gangly at five feet eight and a half and flat-chested, started her own drinking: "With alcohol, I got short, I got breasts. It was total anesthesia." She also had sex and, at fifteen, thinking she was pregnant, attempted suicide. At nineteen, she married a terror: "He'd beat me— nearly killed me. I stayed with him three years!"

During the same years, her father, Paul, a Harvard-educated ad executive and gun fanatic, lost his job, falling into a catatonic depression that lasted eight years. In 1963, when Mariette was twenty-three, he shot himself in the head.

"Mom and I sponged up my father's blood and brains and never mentioned it again! After Dad's death, I reached my drinking bottom, was on the verge of a nervous breakdown. I'd sit on my haunches drunk, eating anything. I was blacking out, hearing gunshots, paranoid and haunted."

"Surrendering was the answer," says Hartley, a longtime devotee of programs such as Alcoholics Anonymous, ACOA (Adult Children of Alcoholics), and CODA (Co-Dependents Anonymous). "Believing in a power greater than myself. I *asked* for help, I learned I'm no longer a victim, that my own fate isn't suicide and alcoholism. I spent twelve years of rich therapy confronting my fear of abandonment, my terror of men. Talking, talking, shedding the shame, the guilt, the secrets, breaking the silence."

Having conquered the nightmare of her own life, Hartley's top priority nowadays is bringing a message of hope to teens prone to suicide.

"I tell my story to groups like KATS (Kids Against Teen Suicide). You should hear what's going on in their homes: drugs, workaholism, sex, coke, alcohol. But teens now have a way out. There are hotlines, therapists, counselors, and I tell them to reach out. Thank God I did."

# MARIETTE HARTLEY

# Couldn't be. This just

couldn't be the same publishing mogul who popped five milligrams of the "upper" Dexedrine into his mouth each morning, who raced through marathon days in his signature silk pajamas, then partied all night—gorging on Pepsi, snorkeling down pipe smoke, and engaging in sexual tournaments.

Hugh Hefner, married and monogamous, with a baby? Please. This is the man who liked to quote Woody Allen: "Marriage is the death of hope."

*Playboy*'s founder and editor in chief says he was a man who "ran and raced" for thirty years, defying his "Methodist-repressed-puritanical childhood" until March 6, 1985. On that night, a blood vessel burst in his brain.

"I was in bed reading headlines out loud to my then-girlfriend," he remembers, "when suddenly I couldn't read at all. I had been incredibly stressed-out for a year, and the next morning, something was drastically wrong with my speech; there was also mild paralysis on my right side—in my eyelid, my face, my hand.

The "second act" of Hef's life had just begun.

"Then, slowly, I *used* the stroke to take stock. During thirty years of freedom, what was I trying to prove? I saw that the 'playboy'

days were my chasing after some new adventure, always just over the hill—attempting to throw off my puritan childhood. I finally realized that sex can be a *part* of love and marriage."

Thus, a year ago, the perennial bachelor—father of *Playboy* publisher Christie and computer programmer David by an early "devastating" marriage that left him embittered—finally took the plunge again. He married *Playboy*'s 1989 Playmate of the Year, twenty-nine-year-old Kimberly Faye Conrad.

"She has an *old* soul," explains Hefner, now nearly seventy, penning his autobiography and fully recovered from the stroke.

"I don't think the disparity in age is going to matter. My mother is going on ninety-five and, like Sinatra, I can 'survive to a hundred and five' . . . if I'm young at heart."

He'll need to be. His youngest son, Marston Glenn, was born on his father's birthday, April 9, 1990.

Hefner calls himself "a homebody" who now believes in monogamy. "Yes, I do, yup. I want to be with Kimberly one year, five years, ten years from now."

And, he says, he's truly happy. "If there's such a thing as a

charmed life, I've managed to live it. Against all odds, I've found renewal—a third act—and made this decade of my life the best of all."

# Hugh Hefner

# Nobody makes an entrance like

was brand
*Letter*, Leo
claimed Q
was found
December
vilified wo

Don
Helmsley,
tising cam
hotel emp
perfection
"vicious."
called her
West." An
Pierson du
Mean."

"Th
Helmsley
loses his te
I'm a push
dent and a
ed and pov
would be t
utive."

In c
something
jade-colore
the Queen
"guilty," g
blade of a
to jail in A

"*Thi*
remembers
tumbling I
hole of mis

Fede
Walker Jr.

Audrey Hepburn. A burgundy cape, the legs of a dancer in chic black silk, the swanlike neck, alligator shoes, rail-straight posture.

No joke that my heart was beating over my rare two-hour lunch with the incomparable Audrey, jetting these days from Ethiopia to Ireland, Turkey, Venezuela, and Ecuador as UNICEF's special ambassador.

Malnourished herself during WW II, Hepburn says, "Now, forty years later, I can get some relief from that knot in my stomach, the pain of watching children starving to death."

With moviemaking behind her, and sons Sean and Luca leading separate lives, Hepburn's happiness pivots around Dutch actor Robert Wolders, with whom she's been living for eight years.

Wolders, the widower of Merle Oberon, met Hepburn at a dinner party in 1981, a get-together that forever changed Hepburn's life.

"I was charmed with him that night, but he didn't register much," she recalls. "We were both very unhappy: Robbie was getting over the death of Merle, and I was in one of the worst periods of my life, the low ebb of divorce. So we both cried into our beers." Over the next weeks, however, Wolders, sev-

eral years younger, began to make an impact: "I discovered that Robbie was solid in every way, and eventually we did fall in love. When that happened, nobody was more surprised than I."

Surprise because Hepburn had indeed become a romantic cynic: "I suppose that's true. I never thought I'd have such serenity, which is very hard to come by, somebody I could trust and depend on. But I'm a romantic woman. What is there without it? Life just becomes so gray."

Hepburn's marriage to Mel Ferrer ended in 1968. "I tried desperately to avoid divorce for my two sons' sake, but I just couldn't." Then she endured heartache from the womanizing Italian psychiatrist, Andrea Dotti: "Your heart just breaks, that's all. But you can't judge, or point fingers. You just have to be lucky enough to find somebody who appreciates you."

And she has: "Robbie is solid in every way, I can trust him. I trust his love, I never fear I'm losing it, he reassures me."

Does their age difference matter? "No. Because he doesn't mind it. If he somehow made me feel insecure because I'm eight years older, then I'd feel it. He doesn't. Also, we're not kids. He's going to be fifty-six. I'm sixty-three.

Marriage isn't needed: "Our answer is why? It wouldn't contribute anything to what we already have."

# AUDREY HEPBURN

# "Ham and cheese. Twelve-thirty."

Click.

Those were the instructions from "Madame," as she is nick-named by one lifelong friend.

In ripped pants, a blue turtleneck, and a red sweater, Katharine Hepburn's still sassy in her upper eighties, having last year completed her bestseller autobiography, titled, simply, *Me.*

Was working on it difficult?

"My work always goes well, and if it didn't I wouldn't tell you."

What lovely dhurrie carpets.

"All for sale. . . . How much will you give me?"

And so it began, an entrancing, seductive, hilarious afternoon in her East Side townhouse with the shrewd grande dame of Hollywood, who carried on a twenty-five year romance with the married Spencer Tracy, a turning point in her life that precluded marriage and children.

From their first film together, *Woman of the Year* in 1942, to *Guess Who's Coming to Dinner* in 1967, Hepburn not only worked with Tracy, but nursed him through his bouts of alcoholism and depression.

"When I met Spencer, everything changed for me," says the woman who in public had to play second fiddle to Tracy's wife—who refused to give him a divorce.

If she has any regrets, she doesn't let on: "Taking certain trails in life fixes it so that you can't take others," she says simply.

"A husband would not have been compatible for me anyway. I was ambitious and knew that I would not have any children. Coming from a big family of six kids, I understood the obligation of time required. I wanted total freedom."

Now, twenty-five years after Tracy's death, surely Hepburn feels lonely at times, it's suggested.

"Nope," she answers, insisting, "there's no greater luxury than doing what you want when you want to do it. I've lived the life I've wanted to."

"Silence," she muses, lambasting Walkmans because they don't let people think, "is pure and true. What's wrong with it? Can't people use their brains?"

So she could recommend living alone? "The most perfect state imaginable," she responds. "The human animal naturally likes company and I *would* be lonely if I were forced to be alone all the time. But I'm not exactly average."

Stoic to the core, Hepburn tolerates a bum hip, a steel rod in her ankle thanks to a 1984 car accident, a longtime eye infection, plus the tremorous shaking of her hands.

"I don't get down, even when I'm sick," she says. "Driving with a flat tire isn't ideal, and I do feel disgusted when I have to crawl up three flights of stairs—but I'm not depressed.

"Now pass the peanuts," she orders briskly.

# KATHARINE HEPBURN

# If one believes that life is

an uncontrollable chain of accidents, then some people are just luckier than others.

"And I believe we make our lives from where we find ourselves," muses Hollywood icon Charlton Heston, describing his career as "a succession of turning points which came together and culminated in a life."

"Statistically you *cannot* make a living as an actor," says the man who incarnated Moses, Ben-Hur, El Cid, and King Henry VIII, among a host of other famous and not-so-famous men.

Born in Evanston, Illinois, in 1924 and raised in the remote village of St. Helen, Michigan, Charlton was a lonely, isolated child lost in his imagination.

"With no TV and only one movie house, twenty miles away, I was a print freak—acting out my favorite stories, *Huckleberry Finn* and *Treasure Island*—because hunting rabbits got boring."

At age ten, what he calls his "idyllic" childhood ended when Charlton's mother, Lilla, tired of country life and divorced husband Russell Whitford. "That was the worst trauma of my life," Heston says sadly, "because it seemed to me that it was somehow my fault—a black mark against me."

When the boy's mother soon after married Chester Heston, Charlton was whisked off to Wilmette, Illinois, an affluent Chicago suburb: "The separation from my father was painful. . . . I didn't see him again until nine years later, when I went overseas to the Army Air Force in 1944. That's a long chunk."

Making matters worse, the traumatized child found himself a pariah at the progressive New Trier Township High School, where he proved himself to be painfully shy and unathletic.

"But," Heston says, "Trier had a great theater group—a happenstance that was terribly fortunate."

Grabbing a drama scholarship to Northwestern University, the six-foot-three hunk was soon tackling lead roles and being heard on radio.

At college, the young actor met the actress Lydia Clarke, whom he married in 1944, after being discharged from the Army Air Force. Then came one of Hollywood's biggest careers.

"Yes," he smiles, "you see how all these things fell into place?

"If my parents had had a happier marriage, and if my mother hadn't remarried, and if I hadn't come to high school with that men-

tal conditioning, and if I had been killed in World War II, we wouldn't be doing this interview."

# CHARLTON HESTON

# "My mother told me years ago

she killed a woman who was 'a bum lady,'" Judd Hirsch remembers. It happened when her electrician husband, Joe Hirsch, cheated on her.

"Yeah, she told me Dad was a womanizing guy, that they fought constantly. When the woman wanted to use *her* pots and pans to cook dinner for him, my mother hit her with a pan and she died." Really?

"Sorry, but *that's* what she says," laughs Tony-winning Hirsch.

Born March 15, 1935, and separated from his father until age ten, the West Bronx Hirsches survived an itinerant existence, "living on welfare in little hovels," says Hirsch, "suffering in dingy walkups—usually about the fourth floor—that were too hot in summer and too cold in winter."

By second grade, the boy had moved thirteen times. "Mom had to keep adjusting to the economy and to what was happening in her relationship," he says. But even after Joe Hirsch returned home in 1945, life with Dad was bleak. "He was a real tough guy—short, very muscular. . . . " And abusive?

"Yeah, I think so . . . violent. What he did then—slapping my face and hands—would be considered child abuse today. My mother feared he might drive me to insanity."

Instead, the athletic young Judd became an "introvert-extrovert," withdrawn at home, rebellious at school. "I was the funniest, most talkative kid on the block—always getting in trouble—but when the kids reacted with laughter, I knew I was being effective."

Also proficient at math and science, the teenager lived with "not a message but a warning cloud" over his head.

"Dad said: 'It's a tough world, you don't have much, you better get a job, better be equipped.' He wanted me to become an electrician." Instead, Hirsch became an academic sleepwalker, first studying physics at City College, then architecture at Cooper Union, then entering the army, then back to City College engineering school—all the while restless and unhappy.

"It was ridiculous. My mind was turning gray. I was *asleep* for a long time because I was always *scared*, a fifties kid—you had to become a *worker* to save your life. To be happy was never taught."

Fate intervened when Hirsch, twenty-one, with "a hole in my program," was obliged to take a theater class to fulfill a humanities requirement. "Total accident. I did a scene from *Night Must Fall* in front of four hundred engineers.

Scary, totally exhilarating because they believed me. I wanted to be on this side of the fence. I wanted to speak, to affect somebody."

The rest, "twenty-eight years of nonstop work," including stardom as Alex Rieger on TV's still-rerunning *Taxi* (1978-83) and the TV series *Dear John*, has yielded a happy life.

Was it destiny? "The more I think about it," Hirsch responds, "the destiny of it, I think, is implanted by a gene called 'what-you-would-have-done-anyway.' My *need* to express myself *had* to come out."

# JUDD HIRSCH

# "In a drawing, I have the

advantage of not being held down by gravity, so I can expand it," exclaims the legendary caricaturist, Al Hirschfeld, perched, as always, on an old barber chair before the scarred wooden drawing table in his townhouse on Manhattan's East Side.

The energetic eighty-nine-year-old, who has immortalized more than three thousand Broadway stars and world figures, celebrates sixty-five years of his works in a recent book, *Hirschfeld: Art and Recollections from Eight Decades.*

"From the day I could hold a pencil, I started to draw—never was interested in anything else," says the artist, one of three sons growing up in St. Louis at the beginning of this century. "My father, Isaac, was allergic to money, never worked," he laughs, "so my mother, Rebecca, a Ukrainian immigrant, was the matriarch, a pioneer lady who ran a candy store."

That was until little Al's art teacher, who lettered price tags in a department store to earn a living, persuaded Rebecca to move to New York lest her son face the same fate.

While his mother clerked at Werthheimer's department store, Al studied at the Art Students League, then, at eighteen, gofered

in the art department at Goldwyn Pictures before moving on to MGM and Warner Bros. as a graphic artist. In 1925, he went to Paris.

"After studying anatomy, sculpture, oil and water painting," he says, "I finally latched onto pure line, and that would stick with me across a lifetime."

His lucky break came in December 1926. In New York, Hirschfeld watched actors Sacha Guitry and Yvonne Printemps perform on Broadway. "I was sitting there with a press agent friend, Richard Maney, and started nervously sketching Guitry on my playbill. Dick said, 'Why don't you put it on a clean piece of paper and let me take it around to see if I can place it?' The next Sunday it appeared in the *New York Herald Tribune* five columns wide and twelve inches deep!"

Luck, Hirschfeld acknowledges. "I absolutely believe in accident. . . . The whole trick is to take advantage of it."

For the next three years, the artist was paid $5 per column width until the rival *New York Times* hired him in 1929. "No contract, just a handshake," he says with a smile, "and that's the way it's been for sixty-three years," years of Hirschfelds that have captured "bigger than life, explosive sub-

jects," he says, like Carol Channing, Ethel Merman, Katharine Hepburn, Eleanor Roosevelt, Winston Churchill, and Marilyn Monroe.

Today, instead of his reproductions selling for $5 per column width, Hirschfeld original pen-and-inks range in price from $2,700 to $20,000 and can be purchased at the Margo Feiden Galleries in New York City.

"Success hasn't changed me," he says. "I sit here all day long, eliminating, whittling each drawing to its bare bones."

And the key to longevity? "No exercise, except in my mind."

# Al Hirschfeld

# The meat-and-potatoes girl

from Houston adored her mother's cooking so much she carried an extra twenty pounds on her five-foot-four frame. But the girth supported a powerful gospel voice that made her popular with boys at the Pleasant Grove Baptist Church.

"My best number was 'He Looked Beyond My Thoughts and Saw My Need,'" recalls singer Jennifer Holliday, who scooped up a Tony and two Grammys for her riveting portrayal of Effie White in the 1981 Broadway hit *Dreamgirls*.

"But as a smalltime girl with good grades, I *really* wanted to be a lawyer and follow in the footsteps of my idol, Congresswoman Barbara Jordan."

That was until, as a teenager, Holliday was accidentally discovered by a dancer appearing in a road company of *A Chorus Line*. She met director Michael Bennett and was immediately signed to co-star in *Dreamgirls*.

"But the more I became popular," she says, "the more isolated and alone I felt. And because of my low self-esteem about my looks and my weight, I couldn't deal with my character Effie's being called ugly." She began overeating to numb her depression, ballooning to over three hundred pounds.

By 1984, she says, "burnt-out" and hoarse from grinding out eight shows weekly, the unhappy twenty-three-year-old left *Dreamgirls*. She anticipated a stellar solo recording career at Geffen Records. While *Feel My Soul*, released in 1985, fell just 50,000 short of going gold, her next two albums failed completely. In 1987, Jennifer Holliday filed for bankruptcy.

"Some people lose their minds when they lose their money. I didn't. I lost my car, my house, my possessions and my self-confidence. The bottom fell out and it was the darkest time of my life. I thought my inability to sell records meant I was a failure. I went home to Texas and lived with my mother."

Then, in 1988, Arista star-maker Clive Davis signed Holliday. She was to make an album of rhythm-and-blues songs titled *I'm On Your Side*.

She tackled her "image problem" in 1990 and lost a whopping 148 pounds on an all-liquid diet. She dropped from dress size twenty-eight to twelve. She even fell in love with Detroit singer Billy Meadows, whom she married in March 1991. Life seemed sweet.

But now it's sour again. The album has fizzled. "I thought I did all the right things," says Holliday, "great quality music, a supposedly number one record company, I lost all this weight—*and I still don't have a hit record.* I wish I knew why."

The marriage also fizzled in divorce after less than a year. "A lot of deception was involved and I divorced him. . . . I thought he really loved me."

Now living with her mother again in Texas and subsisting on so-called track dates—"I sing thirty minutes to music on tape because I can't afford a band"—the still-svelte Holliday, who at 151 pounds is on a thousand-calorie-per-day diet, just started psychotherapy.

"I have to learn how to get self-esteem from the inside—not from outside success. I don't have it yet, but I'm still trying."

# JENNIFER HOLLIDAY

# What a novelty: At a 1938

Democratic Picnic honoring FDR in Bradford, Pennsylvania, a plump four-year-old hometown prodigy nicknamed "Peanut" tackled the stage, unleashing an electric rendition of "The Star Spangled Banner."

"It didn't scare me . . . I liked it . . . and *that* was my very first recital," smiles world-renowned mezzo-soprano Marilyn Horne, now celebrating her fifty-fourth year on the concert circuit.

Born in 1934 and raised by Bentz and Berneize Horne, musical Marilyn was immersed in what she describes as "a boisterous, everyone-yelling-talking-and-singing-at-once household," which included brothers Richard and Jay and sister Gloria.

"At age one," the diva recalls, "my mother says I started *trying* to sing. Six months later, my pièce de résistance was "Walking in a Winter Wonderland," and the rest—seventy recordings, twenty years of curtain calls at the Met—was history. On the home front, her life was forever changed, she says, on September 25, 1978: "That was the day a plane went straight down in flames in San Diego and killed a hundred people," says Horne, "including my brother Richard," a fifty-one-year-old assistant superintendent of public schools in Los Angeles county. "It almost killed

me: I was in Edmonton, Canada, doing *Mignon*, and heard about the accident on the television. No survivors. I lost it, just started *screaming*. Total, total trauma. I don't know about teaching any lessons, but I can tell you the crash was the turning point of *my* life.

"That DID IT FOR ME. That's when I believed in fate, because several things were holding Richard not to get on that plane: His alarm didn't go off, he was late, rushing, his car needed servicing, but I believe he was fated to get on that plane."

Why? "If you have that answer, honey, you'll have a really good article. It isn't an accident. I believe that each person is given a certain *number*, and Richard's number was up."

What comforted her? "For weeks, I got a lot of solace from walking the floor at night listening to the Mahler *Second Resurrection*—plus lots of reading, talking, and therapy."

And singing.

"Right—singing Mignon that night Richard died—the tenor sings: 'Adieu, *Mignon*, courage. . . . 'I mean, I just lost it on stage, but I got through it. My brother would have wanted me to do it. Same thing when my mother died of cancer: The night she died, I sang.

What better thing could I do than sing? I'm always singing through life, and death."

Horne speaks of "At the River," the hymn Aaron Copland arranged for orchestra: "I have this naive thought that Mother and Dad and Richard and I will all be gathered at the river on the other side some day. My mother once said: 'Jackie, I'll be at the river as long as you're singing.'"

#  121 ARILYN HORNE

# The family crown prince—rakish

and rich, the son of a prominent Madrid surgeon—was a cocky one at age twenty. "When you're that age, you're infallible—or at least you think you are," muses Julio Iglesias, then a strapping 187-pound goalie with the renowned Real Madrid Club de Fútbol, with legs of steel and a passion for soccer.

But one night in 1963, young Julio found out how fragile life could be. "I was driving my little sports car very fast," he recalls, "eighty miles per hour on winding country roads about fifteen miles outside of Madrid. Recklessly. Then I turned a curve, lost control, and smashed through the border rail and into a field." The car rolled over and landed on its back. Miraculously, Iglesias stepped out of the car without a bruise.

"I was," smiles the heart-throb, "completely perfect"—until forty hours later, when massive spinal hemorrhaging landed him on an operating table for fourteen hours. He returned home paralyzed from the chest down.

"One day I was a guy full of strength," he says, "the next completely paralyzed. My weight dropped to ninety-nine pounds. I had sex only in my head for three years. I reached down, touched my leg and there was no feeling, no movement. 'Why, why, why, why, why me?'

"At first, I was so, so depressed. I had lost my youth, and felt like giving up because I knew I'd never play soccer again. Then two months later, the day I could move my left toe, I started to grow up."

Refusing crutches or a walker, Iglesias struggled for eighteen months, learning to walk again: "I started to like the challenge of an honest fight—to be better, to gain points, and to wind up stronger.

"One day, my nurse handed me a guitar to exercise my hands as physical therapy." And Iglesias discovered his calling.

"Because I couldn't move for six months, I had become much more alert—more sensitized to colors, sounds, an artistic esthetic—and I starting accompanying singers on the radio, composing songs, singing."

Meanwhile Iglesias regained complete use of his body, earned a law degree, then dropped it cold at age twenty-five after composing "La Vida Sigue Igual" ("Life Goes On as Usual"), which won him a Spanish Song Festival Award in 1968. What followed—130 million copies of seventy-nine albums sold in sixty-nine countries, more than Elvis, the Beatles, or the Rolling Stones—was nothing short of incredible.

"If I hadn't been in the accident, I never would have become a singer," says Iglesias, who rarely takes a vacation from concertizing.

"But it wasn't destiny," he insists. "I can't believe in it—I'm not a determinist. I believe, in fact, in strength, in learning, in *circumstance*. I discovered the most important thing in life is to *not die*." And his fans will tell you: Julio Iglesias lives.

# JULIO IGLESIAS

123

# Actress Amy Irving is still proud of

her former husband, one of Hollywood's richest movie producer-directors, high-flying Steven Spielberg, his net worth conservatively set by *Forbes* at $300 million. "Steven," she says, "is one of the most successful men in the world."

But not at marriage with Irving. Love flew out of the window for the two, and they divorced in April 1989. It was after only four years of wedlock that Spielberg took up with *Temple of Doom* beauty Kate Capshaw, whom he married in 1991.

Left behind was Irving and her whopping $100 million divorce settlement, four-year-old son Max, and a pocketful of reasons for the split.

"*Time* was a big issue with us," says the inactive actress, lamenting that Spielberg became "obsessed" when working on a film. "I had to grab an hour at the end of the day," she says, "and even then Steven was not a natural talker. Also, we were sometimes guilty of paying too much attention to Max and not enough to the marriage. Then we'd try to recoup . . . but it was hard."

"When Steve was filming *Empire of the Sun* in Spain," Irving remembers, "I tended to Max and lost out on roles to other box-office flavors of the months, and I was

going *crazy*. It is the mother," she points out, "who remains the primary parent in our culture, the one who makes the sacrifices."

Arguments also centered on whose career took precedence. "Sure, we had some of that . . . I'm no saint. There were times I would have rather been working than bored in Spain. But my marriage would have been a joke had I been working in another country."

But Irving had to admit that Spielberg was a bigger star, and Irving hated the nepotism of joining forces with him: "No. If I had had a starring role in a Spielberg film, I never would have gotten credit for my own career. I wouldn't fall into that trap. And some producers didn't want a Spielberg ally in their enemy camp. Others thought: 'Who wants her, anyway? She can't be talented if she's married to *him*.'"

Him, him. . . . "Ahh," she sighs, "people are very interested in what he thinks and what he does.

"And so finding my own identity *hasn't* been easy for me."

Irving has since married Brazilian director Bruno Barretto, with whom she has a son, Gabriel. But still, a quiet sadness lingers in the actress because, she says, she entered her first marriage for keeps.

"I didn't believe in exit clauses. No. The exit clause is death. For me, when you say those vows, they're forever."

Money can't buy love, but think of the consolation.

# AMY IRVING

# She's outlaw Jackson, the

family pariah, the wild-card Jehovah's Witness who in 1989 infuriated the Jackson brood by strutting nude in *Playboy*—a boa constrictor her only garb.

Then, in 1990, the loose-cannon singer was penning a tell-all sizzler for Penguin about her travails in Jacksonville, including a chapter about being sexually molested by her father at age ten. Trouble.

"They were trying it again—twice in a week," Jackson whispers, alleging her parents were trying to kidnap her back to the family compound in Encino, California, where this Jackson thriller begins.

Six years ago, at twenty-four, La Toya was still living at home with both parents, imprisoned, she says, in a fantasy world. "Living behind locked gates in seclusion with wild animals and your own movie theater isn't my idea of reality," she says, scowling. "But mother was my best friend. I was the only one there for her."

Being "the accommodating one" rendered her easy prey to the dictatorial Papa Joe Jackson, who masterminded his children's stardom until, one by one, each of the nine left him. "That infuriated my father. 'Control' is definitely the word for him. He was humiliated when Michael and Janet left his

management, because they became bigger stars *without* him."

La Toya wanted to do the same, "but my father said it wasn't important, that I should just stay home until I married. He saw me as a girl of twelve. 'Do this, do that,' was how he treated me."

Three years ago, after a year of begging for release from his management, the patriarch relented and turned his back in disgust. "That was my turning point—leaving my father. I told myself I had to do what La Toya wants to do." *Playboy* included.

"I wanted to do something *bizarre* to stand up and tell my father, 'You don't have control anymore, and I don't need your permission.'"

She looked to her mother for support. "But mother turned on me. I was shocked. I didn't expose my entire body—I wouldn't—and didn't see anything wrong with exposing my breasts. But suddenly, the person I thought loved me so much, hurt me an awful lot. She never calls. . . . "

Then, in September 1990, when Joe and Katharine Jackson learned about their daughter's pot-boiling manuscript, they sprang.

"Who would believe that a woman over twenty-one could be abducted by her own mother and

father? But they showed up at my New York apartment with six in security who tried to push me into a limousine. Inside family sources told me they had a van waiting to take me either to Michael's ranch or to [Black Muslim leader] Louis Farrakhan. I had my own security and they failed. When I called my mother on the phone weeks later, she denied it totally. Since then, they've tried it twice again.

"I thought I knew my mother, but when someone goes so far as trying to kidnap you, something's wrong," she adds. "And it is definitely not over. I keep moving."

Jack Gordon, her husband-manager, also thinks it's scary. "La Toya travels with two armed security who have orders to shoot if anybody grabs for her."

"Hate," La Toya reasons, "is the other side of intense love, and my father has skeletons in his closet. . . . He *is* afraid of that door being opened wide."

# LaTOYA JACKSON

# "You know who got me started

running?" quizzes *Miami Vice* hunk Don Johnson. His calves bulge and his stomach appears rock-solid.

"Paul Newman," he beams, cooling down after a ritual morning run of five miles around his $3.5 million Beverly Hills pad, a nine-room English colonial once owned by Cowardly Lion Bert Lahr.

"Paul is a runner, and back in 1975 he pulled me along one day and I got hooked."

In fact, Johnson considers running, offshore powerboat racing, and lifting weights, "all together . . . the therapies that helped me *back then*." It's a simple reference to his humbling seventies, filled with B-movies, sexual escapades, alcohol, marijuana, and cocaine.

The powerhouse who jogged down the aisle with Melanie Griffith in 1989 for the second time (they were married for less than a year in 1976) describes drugs and alcohol as "an insidious trap," a bottom now replaced with exercise.

"I'm a workout maniac. I pump iron, play sports, ski, play tennis, golf, ride horses, hike, and ride dirt bike. Working out, for me, I've learned, is meditative. I run to get high, but I'm not running because I'm a junkie."

Johnson hates the idea of "giving up" drugs for exercise: "Giving something up is a depriva-tion concept—playing a negative game that sooner or later blows up in your face. I like to think I *went* to something else," leaving chemical addictions, all alcohol, even beer and wine, behind.

"Yup, nothing. I always say God gives you an allotment of alco-hol in life and I just drank mine up early. So it's gone."

Johnson's life is not without risk. In Biscayne Bay, watch out for him gunning his 2,550 HP Gentry Eagle (nicknamed "Mel," for his wife) and racing at more than 100 mph. It's the same kind of racing that took the life of Stefano Casiraghi, husband of Princess Caroline of Monaco.

"If I mess up, I can kiss it goodbye," he surmises. "But racing is not a death wish. I see it as keep-ing my reflexes highly attuned."

Slipping into skintight jeans, Johnson ponders what lies ahead. "I'm at a major crossroads," he admits. "I love being with my daughter [Dakota Mayi], and I'm thinking about moving out of the spotlight, becoming more enigmat-ic. It's tempting."

Five years from now, where will he be?

"Exercising like a maniac, still. Beyond that, I have no idea. I'm turning. . . . I used to say, 'Jesus, the planet Earth is a painful place to be,' and I'd go ahead and kill myself, except I'm too excited to see what's going to happen next." Stay tuned.

# DON JOHNSON

# The single mother on welfare

refused to surrender to poverty after her 1972 divorce: First, she earned a nursing degree; next she changed her name from Diana Judd to the biblically restless Naomi; then, in 1979, she moved her two daughters, Christina and Ashley, from Lexington, Kentucky, to Nashville, chasing her dream of country music stardom.

"Mom was always a warrior for me, a fighter, incredibly brave," beams Wynonna Judd—the once-introverted Christina, who changed *her* name to Wynonna after Wynona, Oklahoma, a town she heard of in the pop song "Route 66." *Voila!* The once-struggling Judds, who had faced countless rejections until RCA signed them up in 1983, blossomed as country's hottest female duo, racking up eighteen number one country hits, ("Love Can Build a Bridge," and "Grandpa"), four Grammys, six gold records, plus the millions.

"It was like hitting the lottery," Wynonna says laughing, "and *performing* together was the closest to flying I'll ever come," though backstage, on the ground, Wynonna relied heavily on her mother's managerial skills: "Mom was 'Miss Know It All,' 'The Queen of Everything,' 'Miss Organization'—her underwear matching her outfits. For eight

years, I could never even find my *shoes*, so on the road she took care of everything," until January 1990, when Naomi Judd was diagnosed with chronic active hepatitis, a sometimes fatal liver ailment that forced her into retirement at age forty-five: "I was devastated. Mom had been sick four years—fatigued, curled in the fetal position, flu-like every day. Seeing her helplessness was *horrible*." So was the wrenching decision to carry on solo after their final concert together in December 1991: "It was death and rebirth. Suddenly I was just another chick singer, didn't feel I had any *identity* as Wynonna. I was in shock, and didn't feel I had the *right* to carry on without her because Mom had worked so hard and I was just 'Naomi Judd's kid.' The *guilt* factor was pretty high because I didn't feel worthy."

Not true. Taking flight with a just-released-and-critically acclaimed first solo album titled *Wynonna Judd*, the youthful star says she's replacing guilt with grace: "Guilt keeps people from advancing," she believes, "and I've erased the word from my vocabulary. I'm learning I have a *right* to go on, a right to be a success on my own, to claim myself as an individual, which most children do much earlier in life."

Was her mother's illness, then, a kind of tragic blessing allowing flight free of the nest? "Yes, absolutely. I never ever would have had the courage to venture out on my own. I've been forced to do this.

"In the studio without Mom," she says in parting, "I was terrified, felt like throwing up. Now I'm trying real hard to see the break as not a tombstone but a stepping-stone."

# WYNONNA JUDD

# The British customs inspector

at Heathrow Airport smelled a poker-faced rat. Sifting skillfully through the high-priced luggage, he found two identical shaving cream canisters, side by side. Each with a false bottom. Each filled with $3,000 worth of cocaine.

"I honestly believe I wanted to get caught," says Stacy Keach, remembering the "horrific nightmare," a $250-per-day habit that landed the actor in London's Reading Jail for six months in 1984, the same year he had hit it big with his CBS series *Mike Hammer*.

"My career was everything back then, and though I was married, I wasn't devoted—had no family values." Even $30,000 a week brought Keach little joy.

"I couldn't accept the success. I felt I didn't deserve it. I had wanted to be an Olivier—a stage actor—not a TV star, someone who sold out, who became a prostitute." The only comfort came from cocaine, says Keach.

"I was not a heavy user. I was a continual user, trapped, convinced I couldn't survive without it. I needed it more and more to repeat the initial euphoria. Cocaine was putting me under in such a state of numbness that I became disillusioned by everything. It took a trauma to change it around."

Heathrow, then jail: "It was a double whammy, two simultaneous feelings—absolute panic and humiliation at being caught at the airport, then total relief. I was fed up with using," and traumatized by his six months in jail.

"The loneliness was agonizing, and I told myself: 'You've wrecked your life.' I was filled with self-loathing. I had no self-esteem until I became the jail librarian. Then I helped the inmates who were illiterate by reading their letters to them. I became almost like a psychiatrist—and felt *useful!* That helped tremendously."

Refusing to hang his head in shame after his release, Keach shared his experiences with Congress—"If I hadn't been arrested, I wouldn't be alive today"—counseled kids against drugs, and otherwise reinvented himself "from scratch."

He smiles: "I'm another person today—so different. First of all, I've never used cocaine again—never even been tempted to go near it in a low moment. I'm lucky. Second, my top priority is my new family," Polish-born actress Malgosia Tomassi and son Shannon. (While in jail, Keach avoided visits from his previous wife, Jill Donahue, and surprised her with a divorce action in June 1985.)

One of his most recent accomplishments was a critically hailed stint as Richard III at the Shakespeare Folger Theater in Washington, D.C. Does he still feel unworthy of success? "Not at all. Spiritual values have come into my life in a very real way. Religion, going to church, praying, surrendering to a higher power. I like myself a lot better because I'm a survivor, because I have gratitude in my life."

# STACY KEACH

# "No phone calls, no

interruptions, no nothing, please," Joan Kennedy implored her loyal secretary, Simone. On a crisp New England afternoon, Kennedy bent over her ebony Steinway drilling herself over and over again on the ethereal second movement of Mozart Piano Concerto no. 21 in C Major, K 467, known as the *Elvira Madigan*.

Just two months earlier, on July 5, 1988, the long-time recovering alcoholic had lost her driver's license for forty-five days after not contesting a drunken-driving citation she received for running off the road near her home at the Kennedy compound in Hyannisport, Massachusetts.

"I made *one slip* in all those years," says Kennedy, who went public with her alcoholism in 1978—"the gutsiest thing I ever did—and people harp and harp on it. They don't give me credit for all I've been through."

That could include the whispered embarrassment of Chappaquiddick, her 1980 divorce from Edward Kennedy, and the agony of watching her oldest son, Teddy, face the amputation of his right leg in 1975, and her youngest, Patrick, suffer from chronic asthma.

But the still-leggy blonde was picking herself up again.

Decked out in pale pink satin two nights later for a charity performance with the Boston Symphony Orchestra and stone sober, she sailed note-perfect through her Mozart, her equanimity a product of spiritual growth. Her performance was a personal milestone.

"Right after the accident," she confides in her only interview since it occurred, "I returned to group therapy, long lunches with *one* woman friend at a time," and most important, buried herself for a week in retreat at a Dominican monastery in western Massachusetts.

"I wore old blue jeans, lived in a cell by myself for three days, and ate meals communally at no-talking tables. In the evening, one monk played the harp, another sang psalms. It was religious, spiritual, and beautiful. I came back to Boston calmer and more centered in myself."

"In fact," Kennedy says, "my inner life is the most important thing in my life, the part of me the public has rarely understood. Jackie and I were the Kennedy wives who treasured slipping away and reading a book on the beach. I believe private time is growth time and feel a profound sense of gratitude for the mistakes I've made because I've learned from them.

"I've learned to *survive*—to keep myself strong and to be myself. That's quite a lot, isn't it?" You bet.

# JOAN KENNEDY

# I got off the radio on February 24,

1987," recalls talk-show monarch Larry King, "and felt a slicing pain in my right shoulder, going down my arm to the elbows. I knew I had a heart problem—was already taking a beta blocker—but I still smoked, never exercised, and ate all the wrong foods. Stupid denial. Although my father died of a heart attack at forty-four, 'it ain't going to happen to me,' I told myself."

Then it did.

"'Mr. King, you're having a heart attack,' is what they told me that night in the emergency room. All the movies are true: the panic, the tubes, the blinding pain. But eight days later, I went home.

"I threw my cigarettes in the Potomac," continues the former three-pack-a-day smoker, and then he waited out the terror of quintuple bypass surgery that would be performed ten months later.

"I absolutely thought I'd die having my chest cut open with a saw, the heart taken out. I told myself: 'I ain't goin' to get up, not me.' I'd die, die. But if you want to know the moment, the turning point," King says, smiling, "it was opening my eyes after the surgery. 'Mr. King, you did terrific!' is what the nurse said. From that moment on, my life changed.

"I thought: If I was lucky enough to live, I'd change, *myself*—

I realized I could have a new life—new energy, new endurance, and feel better about myself."

Gone are the scrambled eggs, pizza, steak, buttered-and-sour-creamed potatoes, Oreo cookies, "and don't forget gallons of ice-cold regular milk.

"Now I'm on the treadmill every day and went from 190 pounds down to 160—and have kept it off.

"I'm over sixty now and feel forty. My eating changed completely—haven't tasted meat since that day, butter, dessert, or pizza. I developed a liking for skim milk, cereals, chicken, turkey, and salads."

Happy at last? "I'm a nine on the scale—still that little Jewish kid from Brooklyn wanting approval from the outside.

"There's no ten. I'd like to have more inner peace. Maybe next year."

For this year, happy birthday, Mr. King.

# LARRY KING

# Attention, perfect-figured

women with money to burn: How about a strapless evening dress paved in gold sequins or sparkling jet from the stupendous fall collection of Calvin Klein?

The kingpin of American fashion offers his usual sublime tailoring, smoldering sensuality, and drop-dead fabrics. Same old Calvin, but not quite.

The celebrated designer used to like modern furniture, bachelorhood, vodka, late nights, and sexually provocative jean and perfume ads with little reference to romance or family values. No longer. Since taking the cure at the Hazelden Clinic—where he bravely licked an addiction to alcohol and prescription drugs in 1988—Klein no longer drinks, he's in bed most nights by ten, he's turned in fun time houses in Fire Island and Key West for antiques and horseback riding in the Hamptons, and commercials for his popular fragrance, Eternity, are all about love between couples.

What's this transformation all about?

*"This relationship has totally changed my life,"* shouts Klein from the hilltops, speaking of Kelly Rector Klein, his super-chic wife of six years.

The story begins eight years ago in Klein's studio, where a

young designer from Connecticut, hauntingly lovely, quickly worked her way up the fashion ladder in Klein's organization. "I get close to everyone I work with," says Klein, "and I used to get very jealous when Kelly talked about her dates. I'd say: 'I think *this* one's not good for you, and I think *that* one's a bad influence—and *definitely* keep away from that one.'"

Finally, surprise! Nobody was left but Klein. "Kelly is very shy, very visual, and very competitive in an athletic way—she has a passion for horses. In a word, she's active—the essence of what a modern young woman is all about. She *is* the Calvin Klein woman," literally so since September 26, 1986, when Klein (divorced from his first wife since 1974) tied the knot in Rome.

"I was very nervous, couldn't believe *how* nervous. My legs were shaking—and I don't *get* nervous. But it's not that often you make *that* commitment."

Commitment, Klein has learned, is the cure-all for a formerly party-prone bachelor: "For all my provocative advertising and my short hemlines, I discovered, in myself, that I'm very old-fashioned. I love spending time in the country, riding with Kelly, time alone

with her, and I now believe in commitment and marriage."

Are we going to see any little Kleins?

"Little Kleins! Well," he laughs, "I *have* one little Klein," twenty-six-year-old daughter Marci, but still. . . .

"Anything's a possibility."

# December 1931: Trekking home

from his hatcheck concession in Newark, New Jersey, Louis Koch—an ingenious and caring father—stopped off at Dugan's week-old bakery for a ten-cent hard chocolate cake and fruit tarts for a penny. Undaunted by the Great Depression, the Polish-born immigrant next visited a fruit stand, and for under a nickel scooped up a pound of soft, slightly rotted peaches, nectarines, pears, and plums. He then headed home to make his famous "fruit soup" for the three kids, Ed, Harold, and Pat.

"Delicious, scrumptious, and I'm still looking for that recipe," laughs gourmand Ed Koch—who hilariously remembers his mother, Joyce, as "a terrible cook who deep-fried everything and burned the veal chops."

Little Ed, no help in the kitchen, was born in the Crotona Park section of the Bronx, December 12, 1924, "a skinny, shy, unathletic, happy little Jewish kid," one unfazed by the poverty that wrecked his furrier father in 1931.

"'*Everybody* was poor, but I didn't miss anything," says the former mayor, who checked hats at age nine, delivered groceries for the A&P at fourteen, chopped liver as a delicatessen clerk at fifteen, and organized a teenage babysitting service at sixteen.

Although he calls being elected New York City's 105th mayor in 1978, "the high turning point of my life, without question," it was David Dinkins's ousting him in 1989 by a slim margin that brought along a new freedom and a change of attitude: "I felt *free at last!* That was a wonderful turning point. Let somebody else worry about the welfare of seven and a half million people and wisely spend a budget of $29 billion fairly, giving up twenty-four hours of your day seven days a week."

"David," he exclaims, "is doing a terrible job," though Koch sympathizes with the stress: "The stress is too great for anyone and my desire to serve the people contributed to my stroke four years ago. So my defeat extended my life." It's a life nowadays crammed with "pure pleasure," he says.

His bankbook is crammed too. The ex-mayor, who earned $130,000 a year, now yearly rakes in $500,000 in lecture fees ($20,000 per lecture), and about $300,000 as a lawyer at Robinson, Silverman, Pearce, Aronsohn, and Berman. And don't forget the professorship at New York University, the WABC radio spot, Fox Television appearances, movie reviews, and a newspaper column.

Koch says his collapse from chest pains at a Manhattan gym in December 1991 was caused by an arrhythmia that has been corrected with a pacemaker.

"Now"—he beams in typical Koch style—"I probably have less chance of dying than you!"

# ED KOCH

# Onstage, Patti LaBelle says,

she's living a dream. Offstage, her life has been a nightmare. The Queen of Holy Roller, Baptist, and Gospel sails across the stage with Cleopatrian panache—resplendent in skintight red velvet and a sequined, spiked coiffure à la Queen Nefertiti. LaBelle's pipes are "driven," she exclaims, "on the gasoline of joy.

"By the end of a show," says the songstress, riding high on her latest album, *Burnin'*. "I'm on another planet," riding an adrenaline high that thwarts the possibility of easy sleep.

"I can't sleep, and don't, until six a.m.—then only for three hours. But when I do wake up, I feel wonderful—and wonder if my sisters felt this wonderful just before they got sick."

For LaBelle, those sicknesses led to a catastrophic series of losses that she discusses for the first time.

"I *was* one of four sisters," she begins quietly, "but Vivien, Barbara, and Jackie are gone . . . all died of cancer." They were forty-six, forty-four, and forty-three, respectively.

"Viv," she explains, "had cancer of the lungs and died in 1982; Barbara had cancer of the colon and died in 1984; and Jackie had cancer of the lungs, which spread to the brain. . . . I lost her in 1989.

"I can't help thinking that I'm next."

"It scares me," admits LaBelle, forty-eight, "though I'm ready for it. I've learned how to suffer by watching my sisters go. They were seventy, seventy-five, and eighty pounds when they died . . . so wasted. . . . Yet right to the end, they were incredibly brave.

"After Jackie's death, I suddenly realized I had never really *told* her, or any of my sisters, how much I loved them, appreciated them.

"And," she says with regret, "there were times I lost my patience when my sister Jackie would complain. I wish I had been more patient."

The loss of her sisters, LaBelle adds, was compounded by her mother's death of heart disease in 1985, and her father's of Alzheimer's disease in 1989.

Her lesson has been a painful one: "But I know it now. I've learned all about tolerance."

LaBelle whispers, "Death has surrounded me—but I definitely believe their spirits are hovering around. My sisters are inside me and I talk to them.

"I've told my husband that I want to go like my sisters did— fighting to the end. I don't want anybody pulling the plug on me.

I'm willing to suffer, and take one breath at a time.

"That," she says, "is because I believe in miracles."

# PATTI LaBELLE

# Growing up in Collingswood,

New Jersey, a skinny thirteen-year-old, five-foot-four, 115-pound shrimp named Eugene Orowitz sweated out gym class, dreading the moment he would be the last to be picked for baseball, basketball, "or just about any other sport," he remembered with agony.

"I was just . . . *there*, but nowhere," said the late actor Orowitz-turned-Michael Landon, "terrible at everything.

"But one day," he recalled, in an interview not long before his death at age fifty-four on July 1, 1991, "I was handed a crummy old javelin in gym class and, though I was the smallest kid, for some unknown reason I could throw it farther than anybody else." Fluke or talent?

"Talent. I was given a gift. I took a slightly bent metal javelin home and started throwing it constantly, working out for hours until my left throwing arm, left shoulder, and left pec became huge."

The boy's confidence was further bolstered that year by watching the film *Samson and Delilah*:

"I saw Victor Mature as Samson with that great long hair and decided to let my hair grow to see if it would help me become stronger. It worked."

By age seventeen, with hippie-length locks, the wiry Landon

had sprouted to five-foot-ten, weighed in at 126 pounds, and had become the U.S. javelin champion, snaring a full sports scholarship to University of Southern California—a crew-cut haven in the 1950s where long hair was considered freakish.

"One day the big weightlifters held me down and shaved half of my head *bald* and put a substance called Atomic Balm on my testicles. I wanted to die. I was just seventeen and it was like being raped." Suddenly, Landon's javelin arm failed him.

"They took my strength away by cutting my hair off," he says sadly. "I felt like an undefeated boxer who just discovered he could be beaten."

Although the teenager practiced until his arm spasmed in agony—without his long hair—his confidence was broken, and so was his left arm: "I was told I would be crippled if I didn't stop. My arm was infected, I had swelling under my armpit, I had torn ligaments, and bone chips were coming out of my elbow."

By springtime he had quit college altogether.

"I got a job unloading freight cars, my hair had come back, and so I had my strength.

"One day," he recalls, "a friend at the warehouse, who was an actor, invited me to an audition. I got the part, he didn't," and the rest is history.

"As devastating as it was getting my hair shaved, it was for a reason," the father of nine believed.

"As I got older, I never stopped believing that my hair was one key element in my success.

"I would have wound up in Collingswood if I hadn't been given that javelin."

The lesson learned: "Don't ignore any kind of minor talent that your kid may have. It may be just the thing the child needs to gain self-esteem."

# MICHAEL LANDON

# "Hard work never killed

anybody," booms Robin Leach, not even a celebrity bloodhound like himself, who tirelessly jets four hundred thousand miles each year in pursuit of gold leaf, stretch limos, and rags-to-riches dazzle.

All of it lands somewhere in Leach's celebrity-guzzling TV conglomerate—*Lifestyles of the Rich and Famous*, in its tenth year, *Runaway with the Rich and Famous*, seven years running, and his brand-new *Home Videos of the Stars*.

But the ever-traveling millionaire, who believes that "everybody dreams the Horatio Alger dream," was once upon a time anything but rich and famous himself.

Born in South Harrow, England, in 1941, the son of an office worker and his wife, Douglas and Violet Leach, Robin found himself on the wrong side of the tracks. "Sir Winston Churchill," he recalls, "had gone to the private school at the top of the hill. I went to council school at the *bottom*.

"I was superindustrious," he says, smiling, "and ran the school 'tuck' shop—the donut, coffee, and soda shop—and the catering service at the swimming pool during the summer, and the class magazine, too."

Leach also religiously wrote an unsolicited column for his local paper, the *Harrow Observer*. "Every

week they printed it—but never paid me, never acknowledged me," until he quit school and asked for a job at fifteen. "The editor said, 'Your desk is waiting. You start Monday.' He was ready for me."

The rest was a quick climb, from the *Harrow Observer* to London's *Daily Mail*, to flipping a coin in 1963 at age twenty-one: "Heads for America, tails for Australia—and you know what came up."

Armed with $133, Leach first sold shoes at Lord & Taylor, then wrote for *Daily News*, eventually spending a decade as show business editor at *The Star* before finding his way onto CNN and then *Entertainment Tonight* in 1980.

Three years later, at age forty-one, "I was reaching one of those crossroads in life," he says, "fascinated by telling stories with pictures, never thinking I'd have my own show, let alone three shows."

But hooking up with TV producer Al Masini—"my mentor, my guide, my business partner"—Leach hatched the idea of *Lifestyles* and off it soared.

"I believe the road map was laid out for me by a higher authority. I also believe the American dream is always alive and well and will never die. I believe our stories

inspire people to literally get off their backsides, pull up their socks, and work hard to achieve success."

Does money equal success?

"It's better to be rich than it is to be famous," he explains. "If you're rich, you can buy anonymity; if you're famous and have no money, you're dead in the water. Neither brings you happiness. You're either born with it or you're not."

# ROBIN LEACH

# Every morning at five,

awakening from restless dreams, a groggy Kenny Loggins would sit peacefully in his bathroom composing words for a song that would radically transform his life.

"*He opened the door and walked away,*" the singer wrote, away from the spiritual torpor of a crumbling thirteen-year marriage to Eva.

"*. . .and from the mountain he could watch it all burn. . . . Welcome friend to the point of no return.*"

The former member of the seventies duo Loggins and Messina was facing a midlife crisis in 1989, when he first separated from his wife and later fell in love with another woman.

"*And all it took,*" he wrote, "*was a sudden Leap of Faith,*" which is the lead song and title of Loggins's intensely personal album.

"It's about embracing change in an active—as opposed to passive—way," says Loggins, "even though change is so terrifying, most people try to dismiss it as insanity."

"Eva and I," Loggins explains, "had been in marital counseling, but the relationship remained distant and adversarial." As hollow, he remembers, as the marriage of his parents—Robert, a traveling salesman, and Lina, a homemaker.

"No true love," he observes sadly. "Their marriage was security-based companionship."

Likewise with Eva, Loggins says. "We were both starving to death." "The Real Thing," another cut from *Leap of Faith*, is written for Loggins's young children, daughter Isabella and sons Cody and Crosby: "I did it for you . . . because love should teach you joy and not the imitation that your mama and daddy tried to show you."

Imitation? "Sounds harsh, doesn't it?" he says with a grin.

"But yes, it was an imitation. I believe in a soul mate." She turned out to be Santa Barbara nutritionist Julia Cooper.

It was she who inspired the album's "Too Early for the Sun": "*I've never known love like this before in my life. . . . I've finally seen my dreams come true. . . . Surrender to the sun, moon, rain, stars, fears, tears. . . . Take a chance. . . . Surrender to love.*"

And so he has. On a tour "that could go on in my life indefinitely," he says, Loggins has had to sacrifice the joys of being a day-to-day father. "My wife and I fought over custody and she won," he says, grimacing. "In my grief over this decision, missing watching them grow is the most painful part. I have weekends and holidays."

Does he have any regrets?

"Let me ask you this," he challenges. "Would it be better if I gave up my career and stayed in L.A.? To have love in your life is the ultimate lesson to teach your children. No longer is true love confused with duty, security or mere companionship. "That's why *Leap of Faith* is so radical," he says. "When I say love exists, that's anarchy."

# KENNY LOGGINS

# Growing up in Garden City,

Long Island, Susan Lucci received double messages from both her dad—tough-guy Italian contractor Victor—and her mother, Jeanette, a nurse of Swedish ancestry.

"My father," recalls the soap opera queen, "treated me like the family brain and believed I could do anything I put my mind to—but he wanted my mind on getting married and filling up a church pew with kids.

"And," she giggles, "when I told my mother I wanted to skip college and move to New York to become an actress, she just threw her body in front of the door, saying: 'You are not leaving this house!'"

So much for a career. But striking a four-year compromise, Lucci wound up studying drama at Marymount College in Manhattan, then afterward going off to modeling agencies and TV soap auditions.

"I was confident, maybe even stupid during those first few months when casting directors told me to forget it. They said blue-eyed blondes and redheads were very good for TV, 'dark' girls bad. I didn't think that applied to me! And 1969 was a very lucky year."

Indeed, in the midst of shooting a B-movie, *Daddy, You Kill Me*, the twenty-one-year-old Lucci turned down thirteen chances to audition for a new ABC soap opera called *All My Children*.

"On the fourteenth invite," Lucci smiles, "I was able to make it and I *got* it," the meaty role of Pine Valley's bitch goddess, Erica Kane, launched in January 1970.

Meanwhile, 1969 had other equally tantalizing gifts for the ambitious actress, who had, two years earlier, been engaged to marry. "Yup. At age nineteen, at a Garden City hotel where I had waitressed, I was sitting at my *own* engagement party when a man I had known as the hotel's food and beverage operations manager walked into the room."

That was the brazen Helmut Huber, an Austrian businessman, who started flirting with the bride-to-be. "Helmut told my mother he didn't think this 'thing' between Susie and this boy was going to last."

It didn't. "Two months later I broke off my engagement, and Helmut started asking me out for breakfast, lunch, and dinner. Very romantic, very persistent. He broke me down and asked me to marry him on the second date. From start to finish, we were engaged in three months."

The couple married in September 1969, and both the marriage and *All My Children* are still going strong.

"When it's right it's right," reasons the wrinkle-free Lucci, still "crazy about" husband-manager Huber and devoted to their children, Liza Victoria and Andreas Martin. Topping it all off, Lucci reigns as daytime's highest paid star, hauling home a yearly $1.3 million.

"I believe in fate, and I believe I was born under a lucky star," Lucci says. "Remember, I missed thirteen auditions for the show; I was married on the thirteenth; my daughter was born thirteen days late; my son thirteen days early. Isn't it amazing? I love the number thirteen!"

# SUSAN LUCCI

# She was Daddy's girl, her big

brown eyes filled with adoration for Dr. Erle M. Blunden, not only an esteemed cancer specialist with his own Sacramento hospital, but a well-to-do adventurer with a passion for taking his baby flying.

"Daddy had a private plane," Joan Lunden recalls, "and we lived in a house—attached to an airplane hangar—built right onto an airfield." But it was not only airplanes that took off from that runway. Lunden's driving ambition, which landed her the co-host's job on ABC's *Good Morning America* twelve years ago, started there as well. In tragedy.

It was 1963. "I was twelve that year," Lunden recalls, "and my father had just bought a brand-new twin-engine plane."

The fifty-year-old physician had owned it three days when "my mother, brother Jeff, and I were supposed to go up with him for a tryout flight. Mom picked me up from school early. But just as we drove into the yard, he was lifting off.

"He waved to me," she says, brushing away tears, "and he never came back."

A few nights later, the thunder of a "terrible, terrible" rainstorm was followed by a knock on the door: "The police told us he crashed full speed into Malibu Canyon as he returned from L.A. with a fellow doctor aboard. Eyewitnesses later reported that the plane went down, then back up, then down again . . . that maybe he had a heart attack."

Suddenly, the doctor's wife had to go back to school, learning the real estate business, her inheritance drained by "the greedy adult children," as Lunden calls them, of the other physician killed in the crash. They sued for $1.5 million, holding the Lunden estate in escrow for a decade.

"After Dad's death, I was never the same," Lunden says.

"It was now the three of us against the world. We felt deprived of a Dad and financial security, and I hated it."

Nowadays earning a reported $2 million yearly and paying former husband, Michael Krauss, $18,000 a month alimony, Lunden is once again rehoning the lessons of self-reliance. The thirteen-year Krauss-Lunden marriage collapsed in January 1992 after a prolonged communication breakdown, their union strained, some say, by Krauss's helping create for Lunden vehicles like the now-defunct *Mother's Minutes, Mother's Day*, and *Everyday*. The hope was that Lunden would have an income independent of GMA. Alas, the

childhood insecurity, though no longer monetary, still lingers.

"I don't want to depend on people who could fire me at any minute," she declares in parting.

"I need to always be in control of my life and my destiny."

Now she is. Stay tuned.

# JOAN LUNDEN

153

# Glaring into the orchestra

pit in a rehearsal for *The Threepenny Opera* at Washington's Kennedy Center in the summer of 1989, Maureen McGovern implored Julius Rudel of the New York City Opera to lower the keys of "Pirate Jenny" and "Barbara Song," her two big numbers.

"But"—McGovern frowns— "I was stuck with a purist maestro" determined to produce an authentic 1928 version of Kurt Weill's score for the much-talked-about Broadway revival featuring rock star Sting.

"Can you imagine," she fumes, "being forced to belt out two songs in the wrong keys for ten-hour rehearsals plus previews at night? Keys are always changed in theater. I begged him to do it, but even after I lost my top octave, he refused to change them more than slightly.

"I finally burst a blood vessel in my right vocal cord one week before opening night, and wound up missing twenty-three performances," she says. It was a puzzling, terrifying trauma for the classically trained singer whose voice could soar over four octaves.

"My God, I'd sung two-hour concerts for twenty years, done shows without mikes and performed music infinitely more difficult, yet those two songs killed me. Nothing but air and squeaks came

out. I saw my life, my living pass before me. Even after the damage was done, Rudel was still reluctant to change the keys. Can you imagine?"

McGovern's next stop was Dr. Wilbur Gould, known as a voice guru by New York opera and pop singers. McGovern says Gould told her she "had the equivalent of a black eye of the vocal cord, and ordered me silent."

So on opening night she passed the gauntlet to her fortunate understudy. "I was sobbing, angry, and devastated," McGovern says. "I prepared for months for the wedding, then missed the ceremony and honeymoon."

Rudel was unrepentant: "Her top octave was very good and she had sung lovely Gershwin," he says, "but in hindsight she was out of her league—miscast. She didn't take instruction very well, didn't know how to handle the songs, and I certainly don't take the blame for her medical problems."

When she returned to *Threepenny* a few weeks later, McGovern, never reviewed, says she finally "forced the maestro to change those keys, by threatening that I would otherwise quit."

And now her four octaves are completely restored. She has two

albums on the way, but she says she lost six months of work. The lesson?

"I will never, never again permit anyone to jeopardize my voice," she vows, "and force me to sing in an injurious key. One show is not worth the rest of my life. And having saved my voice, I'm now willing to use my foot."

# MAUREEN McGOVERN

# The perfume White Diamonds from

Elizabeth, lemonade and popcorn from Paul, a cozy sweater from Calvin . . .

But pining away for a nice movie star to design the interior of your home? Hmm . . . who should it be? Maybe . . .

"Maybe me," exclaims actress-turned-interior decorator Ali MacGraw, who says she detests decorating clichés. "The first thing you should feel when you walk into a home is: 'Ah, I know who *lives* here—not who decorated the place.'"

"My work," Ali says, "includes a starkly modern apartment, an English country house and a very Santa Fe-style restaurant," not to mention her own Pacific Palisades home, filled with Fortuny stamped cotton, antique paisley shawls, kilim rugs, painted country furniture, and turn-of-the-century tortoise bamboo.

For MacGraw, decorating may be a passion, but it's also a necessity, for her acting career has been in semi-park for years.

"I have to work," says the rakish brunette, still with the bangs, who twenty-three years ago grabbed stardom with *Goodbye Columbus*, and a year later, *Love Story*, but thereafter languished in a mere five B-ish movies spread over nineteen years.

What happened to serious roles?

"Ask a studio chief that question," she answers tartly. "The media invented megapop stars like John Travolta and me—the public went crazy—and then the star is squashed. If movies were the center of my life, I would be lovingly slipping through my scrapbooks feeling like hell."

Instead, with her son, Josh, pursuing an acting career of his own, she has turned to representing a cosmetics company, and decorating L.A. restaurants and as many homes as she can muster.

"My life isn't a subtraction, but a multiplication," MacGraw says. "In my fiftieth year, I finally learned that feeling good doesn't depend on getting the next part. I have extraordinary friends, a great kid and wonderful dogs and cats. What else is there?"

Perhaps a movie role? "I agree. I feel that at any moment something bizarre is going to come out of nowhere," she says, "perhaps a wonderful part, or a bad one for so much money I could just laugh all the way to the bank.

"But no matter what, I don't worry anymore. The public usually rediscovers you. So you just have to hang on to your hat and realize that

somewhere between the raves and the vilification lies the truth."

# ALI MACGRAW

# Identically gowned and cooing

"Sincerely" elbow to elbow, Christine, Dorothy, and Phyllis McGuire look like triplets and harmonize as one, but they're as different as sisters can be.

"I'm the extroverted and colorful one, the business manager, *not* the boss but the leader," booms the no-nonsense Phyllis, who now lives on a fifty-thousand-square-foot estate in Las Vegas.

Next, from Scottsdale, Arizona, there's dollars-and-cents Christine, who directed her energies into business after the group's breakup in 1968: "I'm the rebel," she smiles, "and I did what I wanted to do. I don't conform, I don't follow."

Finally, the slightly more sheepish Dorothy: "I'm the follower and peacemaker, and I'm the only one who stayed *married*—for thirty-two years. I'm the family woman."

It was just such differences that broke apart the sisters from Miamisburg, Ohio.

They first hit the big time in 1952 on Arthur Godfrey's show. A decade later, they were raking in $30,000 weekly while crooning out such hits as "Just for Old Time's Sake," "Something's Gotta Give," "Sugartime," and "May You Always."

Why quit? Phyllis: "Chris had just gotten married for a second time and realized her kids had suffered without a full-time mother.

Christine: "We were booked fifty-two weeks a year and although my kids, Rex and David, had *everything*, they didn't have me. I really suffered from guilt."

Offers Dorothy, "My two sons, Harold and Asa, also felt isolated and lonely, and I wanted to spend time with them."

"So," Phyllis picks up, "we just floated away by unanimous consent" until 1988, when the idea of a return was finalized: "We didn't need the money, and it wasn't for ego," says Phyllis. "It was for *need*."

"That's right," says Christine. "Empty-nest syndrome—a double empty nest. My two marriages ended, no love and no children. Double jeopardy."

So, each woman, restless and bored, gave the thumbs up, and the group reemerged at the Bush inaugural in 1989.

MCA later released their *Greatest Hits* album.

"Although I feared a megadose of rejection," says Phyllis, "I'm a workaholic, and producing again was good for self-esteem. Now there's a sense of purpose to our lives, meaning."

"Staying at home is dull," echoes Christine, though the sister

act is anything but. Nowadays jamming twenty hits into forty-five minutes, their stage show—recently dubbed "ageless and brilliant" by the *Chicago Tribune*—includes cleverly crafted medleys of McGuire hits together with salutes to Gershwin, Porter, and Berlin.

"Our voices, thank God, are in excellent shape," says Phyllis with a smile, "but now there's a richness, a mellowness in our sound. Our voices from the fifties grate on our ears. *That* was for teenagers."

# THE McGUIRE SISTERS

# "I do believe in marriage, but

you have to get it right," says former *Tonight Show* sidekick and pitchman Ed McMahon, pushing seventy, who never did get it right, thanks to a furious work schedule that still includes hosting *Star Search*, and cohosting *TV's Bloopers and Practical Jokes* with Dick Clark.

"For years," McMahon explains, "I've been traveling constantly, putting all my energy into my career." It cost him his first marriage of twenty-six years to Alice, a blond beauty he met in 1944. "Everybody was falling in love quickly during the war and heading off to Europe," says the former Marine Corps fighter pilot, who was, he says, "a twenty-two-year-old kid who didn't even know himself."

Fathering Claudia, Michael, Linda, and Jeffrey, McMahon thereafter neglected them: "Almost every weekend I was gone," he admits, "and that was Alice's major complaint. After twenty-six years, we had nothing in common."

A bachelor for the next three years, McMahon was wowed by an airline hostess named Victoria, who became wife number two in 1976.

"With Victoria I got a fresh start, and for thirteen years we got along quite well." The couple even adopted a daughter, Katherine Mary. But then, McMahon said, the curvaceous blonde had an affair with a Beverly Hills cop. "That hurt me, hurt me very deeply. Probably, I wasn't giving her enough attention."

Next, McMahon scooped up another "classy" English blonde named Johanna Ford, and proposed to her on TV during the 1989 Christmas Parade: "I had lost my head," he groans. I was crazy . . . foolhardy . . . but totally sober, so I can't blame it on a drink."

When he canceled the wedding, was it because Ford had contracted breast cancer and had a mastectomy? "Absolutely not. I would have married her in her hospital room, if necessary, but we weren't getting along. We disagreed about *everything*. I called it off."

Then, in February 1991, McMahon fell yet again for a blonde, twenty-six this time, *Capitol* soap actress Andrea Casden—whom he describes as "a long, fun date. She wanted the picket fence, children, the dog, and I couldn't deliver that."

Subsequent to Casden, McMahon fell for a thirty-eight-year-old, still-married socialite, Diana Christie. And you guessed it. "She was a blonde, they've all been blondes, but Diana was closer to my age."

But affable Ed, sixty-nine, actually married a brunette, Pamela Hurn, thirty-seven. "I've learned that a relationship cannot survive if you're only giving fifty-fifty. You need to give at least seventy, no less, and I was never willing to do it."

But he does give to his six-year-old, Katherine. "I give her much more time than I ever gave my older children. She interrupted me the other day: 'Come out and see the snail.' Twenty years ago, I wouldn't have done it. Now a snail is important."

# ED McMAHON

161

# Well, the much-maligned

Georgia Peach, cheek to cheek with The Donald, is now ensconced in one of the Trump luxury high-rises in Manhattan, the dark days of their turbulent romance finally filled with light.

Alas, since the Trumps divorced December 11, 1990, the twenty-nine-year-old Marla Maples has thankfully called a halt to the charade of being "just good friends" with the former billionaire, now on the rise again. And Maples can now marry her man, as she has always wanted to do.

"Donald wanted a divorce, he wanted one for years," reveals the self-possessed blonde, who herself grew up in a broken home. The saga of how that experience affected her begins in Dalton, Georgia.

"It began as a fairy tale," Maples dreamily recalls. "Dad was a junior in high school, great at basketball and football, athletic, the handsomest boy, with a voice like Elvis that could set the girls swooning! Mom was a gorgeous senior, the homecoming queen, with high cheekbones and a Sophia Loren look. They were just meant to be.

"Being an only child," Maples says, "my parents and I were so close, and basic religious values were pushed on me at an early age." She recited the Ten Commandments every night.

"I thought the worst thing that could ever happen would be my parents' splitting up." And by her sixteenth birthday, the worst thing had happened.

"Dad came in my room and said, 'Your Mom and I really need to separate because we're not getting along.' Dad had built our dream house and was buried in bills paying for it, while Mom was turning forty, feeling lonely, and wanting him home more. I said, 'But Dad, the Bible says, "You shall not inherit the kingdom of God if you divorce."'

"But the marriage," Maples adds sadly, "was killing him.

"At first, I blocked out the pain. For a Bible-fearing girl I had to rethink my whole faith. I went deep inside and worked out my true feelings about God—developing my own spiritualism. By eighteen, I finally realized that my parents were good people, that God was not going to condemn them."

Nor would He condemn Maples for falling in love years later with a married man.

"I've learned you can't take the Bible literally and be happy."

And what has she learned from her experience being portrayed as the "other woman"? "We have a long way to go as a human race," she says, flattered and

appalled by the deluge of publicity. "I didn't break up the marriage," she insists stonily, declaring, "nothing is black and white."

"I believe in marriage *and* monogamy," she finishes. "I want it [marriage], but marriage on a *soul* level. That's what Donald and I have." A soulful Donald? "More than you'd expect," she smiles. After walking through fire, the couple deserves the happiness and peace they finally have found.

# MARLA MAPLES

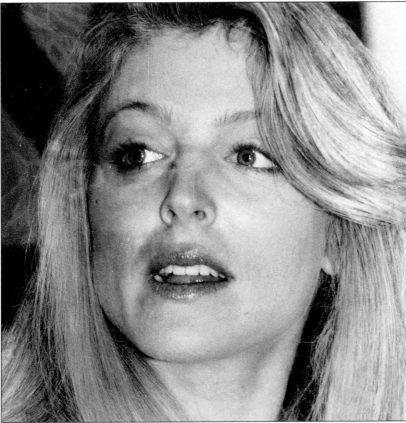

# Jackie Mason went bankrupt nine

years ago, wangled his way out of a palimony suit, and considered himself a second-rate star until 1986, when *The World According to Me* earned him a Tony and a mountain of rave reviews for his one-man Broadway show.

Although his 1989 sitcom, *Chicken Soup*, sank like a leaden matzoh ball, the plump jokester will soon tackle Broadway again, a sellout assured.

But what were the chances of such exposure seven years ago?

"My sister-in-law, who has been unemployed for twelve years, would have had a better chance than me," says Mason, remembering the tumultuous events that nearly relegated him to depressive oblivion.

The rabbi-turned-joker was on the road to major stardom when discovered by Ed Sullivan thirty years ago. "I was a hot number then—the classiest little Jew—until the finger incident," he says, a bitter reference to Ed Sullivan holding up two fingers warning Mason to wind down his act, and Mason allegedly pointing a finger back.

"I *didn't* do that, but Ed was the Pope then, and an hour later my career was wrecked. I suddenly became a filthy person, the dirtiest Jew in the country," who nonethe-

less went on to earn a respectable $400,000 a year in nightclubs.

"Major stars *don't* make $400,000," says Mason.

"I was like a guy running for president, who suddenly finds out he's only a senator. Hubert Humphrey never got over it."

Mason has gotten over it. He is now raking in $4 million a year, and charging $65,000 per club date, not his former $7,500.

"I'm in a state of shock. It's a fantastic relief. I'm like Bush taking the oath of office. Before getting elected, he looked frantic, tense, turbulent. Now that he's got the job, his whole life is getting a tan. Hostages or no, he still looks relaxed."

"I would say," Jackie tells me in parting, "that this is the unlikeliest of times to suddenly become a hit. Yet George Burns revived at eighty."

Then why was *Chicken Soup* such a megaflop?

"Joe DiMaggio was the greatest hitter of all time, and he only hit one out of four balls. If you don't try, you have no chance. If it works, you thank God."

# JACKIE MASON

# A three-year-old named Lucy

Ann Collier was startled one afternoon in 1926 when she heard a man's voice within her head.

"Lucille . . . Luciiiiiille," it said. "*Listen* to me . . . I'll be with you always."

"*That* was my guiding spirit," remembers Ann Miller, the girl with rickets and knock-knees who transformed herself into MGM's tap-dance queen—a queen blessed with a special gift from that day forward.

"I am a psychic," declared Miller, author of *Tapping into the Force*, a personal memoir about reincarnation and the spirit.

"I'm also clairvoyant—I've led many lives. I danced as Egypt's Queen Hatsheput in 1485 B.C. My great-grandmother was a full-blooded Cherokee Indian—one of the greatest psychics. She could put out her hand and move a chair across the room. I saw her do it. She said I would inherit some of her power."

That power became most critical in 1981, when Miller's mother was dying. Miller had depended on Clara Collier for nearly everything, as her three short-lived marriages were "disastrous."

"Yup. First husband pushed me down a flight of stairs and broke my back, second one broke my arm, third one died. So it was just

Mother and I. We lived together. She was my companion, my sister, drove the car, took care of the pups. She'd cook, answer fan mail, was my business manager . . . an incredible woman."

But arteriosclerosis, three strokes, and three hip operations had nearly ended it all for the eighty-nine-year-old.

"Finally, Mother was in a coma and the doctor told me she'd never recover. He recommended that he pull out the plugs. I then put my antenna up and called upon my spirit: 'You've got to talk to me because I'm in terrible, terrible trouble. What am I going to do?' And the voice said: 'No.' I held Mother's hand for two hours and felt her subconscious mind working. I said: 'Come back to me, come back, come back.' She finally opened her eyes and said, 'Hello, baby.' My mother lasted for six months after that!"

Her mother's death hasn't stopped Miller from communicating with her: "She comes to me. I can *feel* her, sometimes I smell roses when there aren't any flowers in the room. My voice tells me: 'Your mother is here with you and she's well.'

"I'm now convinced that only our bodies die—that the electrical spark of your spirit shifts into

another dimension," says Miller. "I know Mother will be waiting for me. So I'm not afraid of death."

# ANN MILLER

# Single? Forget cocktail

parties, dating services, and blind dates. Try a hospital.

"It happened to me," says Mary Tyler Moore, remembering a panic-stricken night eight years ago when her mother was hit with chest pains. "It was Yom Kippur. My mother's doctor was unavailable, so we were sent to a Dr. Levine at Mount Sinai Hospital."

"Oh God, here was this tall, handsome gentleman who was treating my mother so sweetly," she remembers, and instantly the superstar actress, then forty-six, was smitten with the thirty-one-year-old cardiologist.

"I said to myself: 'Maaaary, you ought to be ashamed of yourself,'" but two house calls later she no longer dismissed the inevitable. "On his last visit, he said if we needed him for any reason at all, we shouldn't hesitate to call. So I said: 'Does extreme loneliness come under the heading of emergency?'"

With her divorce from Hollywood producer Grant Tinker three years behind her at the time, Moore says, laughing, "I was aggressive, pushy, and persistent. Robert later told me he was scared of me. I *had* to be pushy because he wouldn't take the initiative."

The affair that followed turned serious. Did he propose? "No, I did. I felt we were ready to marry and he did too, though he was concerned about how his family might feel."

Was an older, Catholic, twice-divorced star what a Jewish mother had in mind for her son? "His parents liked me, but they had a hard time getting over their stereotypical notion of what Hollywood people are like."

The marriage works, she declares. "I'm more open with him, expect less of myself, and I'm less of a perfectionist," says Moore. "And for the first time in marriage I have an equal say. I finally have grown up and don't need guidance or leadership from a father; what I needed was a loving, best friend—that's Robert."

Moore chides skeptics who raised eyebrows when she married a man fifteen years her junior: "It works just fine. No matter *what* we do," she says, flashing that inimitable grin, "our physical energies are well-matched." So there.

# MARY TYLER MOORE

169

# At Paul Newman's jazzy Fifth

Avenue penthouse, a Mozart piano concerto sets the mood. In an intimate study decorated with a carpet of wild tigers and paintings of exotic birds ("One of my daughters is studying to be an ornithologist," he says), Newman showed off two centerpiece pillows embroidered in bold letters: LIVE LONG ENOUGH TO BE A PROBLEM TO YOUR CHILDREN and FOR A WONDERFUL FATHER.

The movie icon is no ordinary father. In fact, despite his many accomplishments, the wiry Newman talks shyly about a turning point about a decade ago, when he realized his career had made him a uniquely problematic dad. "It hit me that I had no natural talent to be a father. Period. That's an objective fact," he says.

"In fact, I had no natural gift to be anything—not an athlete, not an actor, not a writer, not a director, a painter of garden porches—not anything. So I've worked really hard, because nothing ever came easy to me."

What could he have done better as a father? Newman laughs: "Ask my children," Elinor (Nell), Melissa (Lissy), and Clea—his three daughters with Joanne Woodward—and from his first marriage to actress Jacqueline Witte, Susan, Stephanie, and Scott.

"They're all handcuffed to their beds just down the hall," he jokes.

"There are," he declares, "about one hundred eighty thousand liabilities to having me as a father. Some of my children have been more aware of the liabilities than others." Newman adds, "One liability, I realized, is that there's always an element of competition between children and their parents. It's unavoidable."

Newman's only son, Scott, was an aspiring actor who died in 1978 at age twenty-eight from an accidental drug and alcohol overdose.

"Tell your kids," Newman says soberly, "that being a free agent, a responsible one, is what's cool, that you can get as much enjoyment out of saying no as from saying yes. Parents can't supply their children with utopia. But they can help them realize you can feel good without drugs."

Newman pooh-poohs prescriptions for happiness. "I don't even think about it. You can't take a pinch of oral sex and mix that with two batches of popcorn and one steering wheel and have automatic happiness. Life is not a recipe."

On the other hand, speaking of recipes, Newman signs off with

his assurance that he makes the best hamburger in the United States.

"Use only ground chuck, have your butcher put it through the grinder twice instead of three or four times; do not, I repeat, do not, pack the meat too tightly into a ball—it must breathe. The patty should then be cooked an inch and a quarter to an inch and a half thick, it must be cooked over charcoal, it may never be turned but twice and should be served medium rare. Nobody who's ever tasted my hamburger can remember eating a better one. Also, at my house, it comes with a bottle of 1961 Lafite. Who's going to quarrel with that?"

# PAUL NEWMAN

# Trapped in the poor prairie

town of Ryan, Oklahoma, Carlos Ray Norris was a lonely, insecure boy who had moved sixteen times by age twelve.

Adding to his insecurity, the introverted youth was traumatized by his father, Ray Sr., an alcoholic who would lie in a stupor for days on end. Making matters even worse, the unathletic boy was beaten nearly every day by bullies.

"According to society's standards, I was a total loser," says kickboxing film star Chuck Norris, who especially likes his film *The Hitman*, a karate-cruncher featuring a complex character he describes as "a supposedly vicious, calculating undercover hit man, who befriends a fatherless kid—a kid also chased home every day by a bully. . . .

"My school had one Indian kid who followed me home past a gas station and beat me up every day," Norris recalls. "One day, the gas station guy couldn't stand it anymore, stopped me, and made me turn and *fight* this boy. That was the first turning point of my life.

"What the mechanic told me stuck with me all these years: *Running from your fear is more painful than facing it*. I never ran again," except toward excellence.

In 1958, straight out of an L.A. high school and determined to be a cop, a lean and weak Carlos

joined the air force, determined to beef himself up with judo.

"I had to work harder than anybody else as a karate fighter to turn around my insecurities as a man," says Norris, nicknamed Chuck by air force buddies. "Judo," he says, "became the most important thing in my life," and from 1968 to 1974, Norris reigned as world middleweight champion while opening a chain of his own karate schools.

But by 1971, the schools had dragged him into debt. "It took me five years, every dime I had in my savings," he remembers, "to pay off $280,000. By 1977 I had no money, no job," but encouraged by former karate student Steve McQueen to pursue acting, Norris banged on "a thousand Hollywood doors" offering his roughly self-written script called *Good Guys Wear Black*.

The effort was produced in 1978 for a measly $1 million and racked up $18 million in profits. Twenty films have been made since then—including such Norris classics as *A Force of One* (1979), *Code of Silence* (1985), and *The Delta Force* (1986).

"I believe in fate," Norris says. "I believe we're predestined in a certain sense. If my schools hadn't gone broke, I wouldn't have, in des-

peration, turned to acting. A catastrophe can be a blessing because when one door closes, another opens."

Married for thirty years to Dianne Holecheck, whom he divorced three years ago, Norris is nowadays floating in space, lovewise: "It's actually scary being single again, like working without a net, but I like a challenge. I want a relationship and it could be around the next corner. That's the lesson of my life: 'Don't give up!'"

# CHUCK NORRIS

# An avalanche of heartache had

buried her soul, suffocating Dolly Parton's natural ebullience. So one afternoon, alone in her bedroom—recovering from a hysterectomy and forty-five pounds overweight—she eyed the gun in her nightstand drawer, contemplating suicide.

"I was sorrowing, depressed . . . *very* low," she whispers. Then her dog, Popeye, came bounding up the stairs, his eager paws jolting her back to reality.

Parton suddenly froze, then prayed, believing Popeye was a messenger from God. "I thought, 'I'm too chicken to kill myself—so why don't I *juuust* get up and do something about making things better.'"

The story begins in 1982. "My hardest time," Parton reckons. It was the year she made the widely panned *Best Little Whorehouse in Texas*, with Burt Reynolds.

"Makin' that movie," she says, "was nothin' but heartache, a bloodbath. I was already sick with female problems—my hormones were out of whack and I was hemorrhaging. Also, Burt was in a bad place [said to be throwing tantrums that brought Parton to tears] all because he was gettin' over his heartache with Sally Field."

Then, in September 1982, Parton collapsed at a concert in Indianapolis. "I went on, just got dizzy, weak, and fainted right on the stage."

A partial hysterectomy threw Parton into a deep depression. "For about six months I woke up every morning feeling dead," she remembers. "Thank God, I didn't want children real bad, though having the operation was emotionally difficult anyway."

Finally, one day, "the light (and Popeye) came into my room." She smiles. "I was angry . . . at myself and told myself: 'You're either going to blow your brains out or *get off your fat ass and lose weight and get into a better place in your mind.'*"

Ever since, Parton—who slimmed down from 165 to 105—has been aflight, onscreen and off, running her very own theme park, Dollywood, plus Sandollar Productions and The Dolly Parton Wellness and Rehabilitation Center.

"Now I've got *lots* of energy." Looking back, she says, "I needed to take an inventory of my life. I can never allow evil to get ahold of me again." She's now penning a series of positive-thinking books based on what she calls the "Individual Awareness Method."

"I'm trying to help build people's confidence and show there is hope—and I want to be a light, I want to shine, and I hope my shinin' helps somebody walking in shadow."

Keep shinin'.

# DOLLY PARTON

# The exuberant three-year-old,

a charmer from birth, climbed into his grandmother's lap one summer day in 1938, humming an Italian nursery rhyme to her. "One day," she told him, "you're going to be great . . . you will be . . . you'll see. . . ."

"Doesn't every grandmother say that?" laughs megastar tenor Luciano Pavarotti, remembering his days growing up in the Po River Valley of Modena, Italy, "a place," he smiles, "where I learned to be happy."

As a boy, young Luciano reveled in soccer, buried himself in the family's hefty record collection, and listened to his father, Fernando—a baker by trade—sing in the local church. On Luciano's fourth birthday, a remarkable musical odyssey began.

"Almost immediately, the musical talent began to show itself," he recalls. "I was a brilliant boy, very naive, but brilliant." Vocally brilliant? "No, no. Brilliant in character, in communication with people. I was a bad student, some B's, mostly C's. But I was an excellent boy alto."

His mother dreamed he'd become a banker. "Instead," he explains, "I taught elementary school in my early twenties, but my father constantly goaded me, said I was wasting my time, singing

below my potential." The young man, at twenty-two, dumped teaching for selling insurance, to give him enough time to develop his vocal talent. "Studying voice, and studying it with Arrigo Pola—that was the turning point of my life," the opera star reckons.

"My teacher was a tenor and made me learn by example. That was luck, because by imitation I was able to do in two days what would have taken at least two years. When you reach for certain notes the first time, the voice is strangling, and I could not believe that was right, but I was convinced when I heard the results. From Pola, I learned all the technical baggage that I carry with me now. He released the talent."

Released it indeed. In 1961, at age twenty-six, the young tenor won the Concorso Internazionale, a regional competition in Italy, upon which the singer began a formidable European career. Today, thirty years later, he remains one of the highest paid, most visible opera singers in the world, who will be forever known as the person most responsible for popularizing an art form formerly reserved for the elite.

"I've learned it's a mistake to take the safe path in life," says the six-foot tenor, who admits to a constant struggle to keep his

formidable weight under control. He's traveling this fall from Covent Garden to Rome to Florence before landing for Christmas in Modena, still home for his wife of thirty years, Adua, and their three daughters. "If I hadn't listened to my father and dropped teaching, I would never be here. Then, my teacher groomed me, but no teacher ever told me I would become famous. Just my grandmother."

She left him with a lesson: "'Love people, no matter what your occupation.' Sometimes, when I feel strange standing onstage, I ask myself: 'What is little Luciano *doing* here?' I'm loving people—that's the key."

# LUCIANO PAVAROTTI

# He was hungry for autonomy and

big-time Oprah bucks. He was also sick of *A Current Affair*'s over-the-edge sensationalism. So ambitious Maury Povich ditched Fox and press baron Rupert Murdoch and took up with Paramount. Voilà: *The Maury Povich Show.*

"After five years I was getting cabin fever sitting behind that desk," says the news-snooper, who vacated the highly rated *Affair* niche for a new show.

But this is a risk typical of a man who wanted to be "Lenny Bruce as anchorman," as he wrote in his autobiography, *Current Affairs: A Life on the Edge.*

"I originally wanted to be a professional baseball player," says the anchor, whose father was esteemed *Washington Post* sports columnist Shirley Povich. "But I gave up on that when I was sixteen and did the next best thing by elbowing my way into journalism."

He moved to TV and bounced from station to station for years until he attained a secure position at WTTG in Washington, D.C., hosting *Panorama* from 1967 to 1977, then again from 1983 to 1986. But he became better known as the husband of newswoman Connie Chung, until Rupert Murdoch thrust him into the national spotlight as anchor of *Affair* in 1986.

What followed was, he says, "a roller-coaster ride through the dark corners and gaudy spectacles" of tabloid news.

"The up side was the show put me on top and saved me from being Mr. Chung; the down side was looking at the tragic side of life."

Finally, having "conquered the mountaintop," Povich jumped at hosting a conventional talk show, "because all anchors, including Walter Cronkite, suffer the same fate: getting fired. Cronkite was left in the dust, put out to pasture. I wanted to leave on top. This was the ultimate challenge."

But there's one more. The Poviches still want to fulfill their dream of parenthood: Chung cut her commitment to CBS so she and Povich could "aggressively" pursue the subject.

"I want a baby as badly as Connie does," says Povich. "Then," he smiles, "she can go back to work and I can stay at home. That would be my *greatest* success."

# MAURY POVICH

# A few minutes before midnight,

after a long night at the library, the studious college freshman with the long auburn hair threw her books into the backseat of her baby—a chocolate-brown Mustang with vanilla racing stripes—and headed home.

The lovely eighteen-year-old—a cautious girl who had given up teenage dreams of acting to learn the art of healing—felt exhausted after twelve hours of cracking books at Dade Junior College, though she was alert this night, focusing her luminous brown eyes on South Florida's I-95. Her quiet life was about to explode.

"I was suddenly hit," Victoria Principal remembers. "I would later find out the guy was doing double the speed limit—plus he was drunk.

"He finished my college career and almost my life," says Principal, who has never before discussed the ensuing tragedy: "It makes me very uncomfortable. It's like taking a ride at Magic Mountain except the ride doesn't come down properly. As we talk about it, I'm getting an upset stomach. People in bad accidents usually fade in and out of consciousness with flashes of remembrances.

"But I was," she whispers, "very unfortunate—conscious the

entire impact time. I wish I *had* blanked out," which she did by the time an ambulance arrived with a priest, who administered last rites. "Nobody thought I'd survive," says the woman who hovered between life and death for a week and then spent twelve months recuperating.

"Physically I was over it in a year, but emotionally my attitude toward life as an eighteen-year-old was transformed. It was the turning point of my life. Suddenly, I was a teenager with a sense of mortality," and thoughts of being a chiropractor vanished.

"I packed up and moved to New York to pursue acting. From that day forth, I felt I didn't have any time to waste, no time for a fall-back position, because life was so fragile. Any day, somebody else could come along and hit me. I had to pursue my dreams."

Eventually, those dreams came true via an "ecstatic" marriage to Beverly Hills plastic surgeon Harry Glassman, plus nine years on *Dallas*, followed by Principal's emergence as a producer of such TV movies as *Scandal Kills*, *Nightmare*, and *Dance With Death*.

Her own dance with death has never been forgotten. "I've learned that life is a combination of happenstance and destiny. I could have died that night, but I didn't."

"Still," she finished, "I don't drive on freeways. I wish it would leave me . . . the fear . . . but I'm so uncomfortable driving. I feel like my life is in the hands of those surrounding me, so I just don't get on them—never did after that night."

# VICTORIA PRINCIPAL

# Sally Jessy Raphael's

daughters, Allison and Andrea, self-professed cosmopolites, looked at each other half-smiling, like Baby June and Louise in "Gypsy."

"Oh noooo, she's at it again, she's fired, we're moooving" was the refrain, as their report cards whirled from White Plains to Hartford to New Haven to San Juan to Miami to Fort Lauderdale to Pittsburgh—nine schools, thirteen moves, eighteen jobs in all for . . . Mama.

Mama was sinking in debt, the "monkey of broadcasting" strapped to her back with no decent job in sight.

"Oh God, it was horrendous," moans the Emmy-winning talk show host, who's squired around these days in a Lincoln limousine.

But twenty-five years ago, the family of five—business partner-husband Karl Soderland, his two daughters, Sally's two girls and the couple's adopted son, JJ—sometimes slept in a beat-up car, their dinner a dollop of ketchup on crackers.

"When we were in an absolute state of disaster, Karl waitered in a seamy Italian restaurant while I was living off credit cards. But," Sally adds, proudly, "I would not give up."

Why not? "I knew I was good . . . though Lana Turner sip-ping a soda I wasn't. God certainly took his time and," she adds, "one loses faith. I became overly cynical."

But she persisted, to the point where in 1982, finally coasting nicely with her own nightly syndicated radio show, Raphael was invited onto a second-rate TV talk show in Cincinnati. She met the show's executive producer, Burt Dubrow. He became her savior.

"I'd never heard of her," deadpans Dubrow. "I thought Sally Jessy Raphael was three people. She guested on my show and was dreadful. She was boring, had nothing to say. The *second* time, she relaxed and was wonderful—not overly attractive, not threatening, but smart!

"Suddenly," Dubrow adds, "women over forty were becoming very attractive. Yet there was no woman counterpart to Phil Donahue."

There is now.

The cynic couldn't believe it: "I was always hoping against hope that somebody really meant it. Burt meant it and delivered. I give him the credit."

It was the all-nurturing Dubrow who helped Sally through the traumas of 1992: First her son, Jason "JJ" Soderlund survived a near-fatal car accident in January; then her daughter, Allison Vladimir, died in February from an accidental overdose of a combination of prescription and over-the-counter drugs.

"Burt has been a true-blue friend in every sense of he word," says the now-revived star: "He helped me arrange the funeral and while doing that kept our show afloat. But most important, Burt knew when to comfort me and when to leave me to myself."

Back to normal and seen in 190 markets, a bittersweet Raphael is filled with gratitude for her professional blessings: "Oprah goes on the air and a month later she's the biggest thing that ever walks the face of the earth. It took me seven years to get here . . . but. . . . hallelujah! I'm very lucky."

# SALLY JESSY RAPHAEL

# One day nearly eleven years

ago, Lynn Redgrave sat in her dressing room, her red robe open, the clanking of grips and cameramen shut out, nursing her newborn, Annabel, while studying her lines for the then-CBS hit series *House Calls*.

"Either leave the baby at home or quit the show!" is what a male negotiator without children told me," the actress recalls of that momentous day. "I was furious, frightened, and horrified."

"What kind of an SOB," she queries, "would deny a mother breast-feeding her child?"

That 1981 dismissal from *House Calls* set into motion a crusade that sidetracked her career and sent her into the courts and to Congress.

"Suddenly," she exclaims, "I was battling the world," undertaking, with her husband-manager John Clark, an obsessive and steaming battle to win $10.5 million from Universal and MCA studios, which continues unabated to this day.

Universal spokesmen insisted the breast-feeding flap was only a foil for demands made by Clark, who "wanted her salary doubled and development funds for their production company."

"Not true," insists Redgrave. "It was never about money, though

I haven't won a penny in damages, nor have I received an apology." However, she hasn't starved either. She's spent $500,000 of the money earned for regularly flinging off her red chiffon "fat dress" in Weight Watchers commercials to make a point.

"It's my right to do whatever I damn well please in my own dressing room. Nobody ever yelled about the *ladies and noxious substances* that have disappeared into a great many male dressing rooms—and they're worried about a baby slowing down shooting. Ridiculous!"

Redgrave became a star witness at congressional hearings on child day-care: "I made it such an issue that no producer would now dare risk a lawsuit preventing a mother access to her baby at work; and Warners, Columbia, and NBC have begun a combined day-care center.

"But Universal still doesn't have one—we have only six hundred companies in the U.S. that offer women day-care."

Redgrave thinks she has paid a price for pointing out such facts: "I've made two movies in ten years. I'm viewed as a troublemaker."

All this, the actress says in parting, "has made me stronger because I came to grips with the

fear of never working again, and have come out on the other side."

# LYNN REDGRAVE

# "You are sixteen, going on

seventeen, baby it's time to think
. . . . Better beware, be canny and
careful, baby you're on the brink
. . . ."

"And I was," grins
Christopher Reeve, drifting back in
time to the year he was sixteen
going on seventeen in Princeton,
New Jersey, a heady time for the
varsity hockey-soccer jock who
played in Turgenev's *Month in the
Country* that summer of 1969.

A year later, buried in his
theater studies at Cornell
University, the six-foot-four-inch
Reeve discovered a letter plunked
on his desk.

"You may not be interested
in an agent," wrote agent Stark
Hesseltine, the New York Svengali
who had discovered Richard
Chamberlain, Michael Douglas, and
Robert Redford, "but should you
ever happen to be in New
York. . . ."

The young man's eyes
bugged out: "I couldn't quite make
it the *next* day," Reeve jokes, "so I
waited forty-eight hours."

"You're very good-looking,'"
the agent told him, "but you're
much too tall for films." He therefore launched Reeve, after seven
years of grooming him for the theater, opposite Kate Hepburn in *A
Matter of Gravity* in 1976. The following year, Mr. Agent ate his

words by insisting that his
"scrawny" client audition for
*Superman*. The rest, as they say, is
history.

For sixteen years, "I never left
Stark for another agent, never
turned my back on him," says
Reeve, who was crushed when his
"anchor," he says, contracted AIDS
in 1985.

"That was devastating to me
. . . . I didn't know what AIDS was
. . . . I desperately wanted to visit
Stark in the hospital, but, back then,
there was terrible shame attached to
the disease and he requested that
his friends not come. He hated the
way he looked . . . so wasted."

Soon after Hesseltine died in
1987, Reeve became one of
Hollywood's most outspoken
activist fund-raisers for AIDS
research, against the advice of some
Hollywood bigots.

"People told me that a heterosexual movie star like myself
should be careful . . . people would
think I was gay. I told them to stuff
it. When you see babies and mid-
dle-aged women die of AIDS, you
realize the disease cuts across all
segments."

From Hesseltine's death,
from the tragedy of watching
twelve more friends die of AIDS,
Reeve says he has learned a powerful lesson.

"I don't take anyone for
granted anymore . . . friends can be
suddenly taken so quickly . . . in six
months . . . gone. So I try not to
waste time: I say what's on my
mind and reach out, hoping to
make every second count."

# CHRISTOPHER REEVE

# Adrenaline pumping, euphoria

soaring, the Alabama 'flight machine,' as Lionel Richie nicknamed himself, was near-invincible, with nine consecutive years of number-one singles, five Grammys, an Oscar, and a $100 million bank account. In fact, Couldn't-Slow-Down Lionel was downright dizzy with joy from "Dancing on the Ceiling," until March 1987, when he crashed to the ground. "Suddenly, my whole world was coming not a *little loose*, but *totally unglued*," says the Mystery Man, now awakening from hibernation after a whopping five-year hiatus sparked by the collapse of his seventeen-year marriage, the death of his father, Lionel Sr., and a previously undisclosed series of throat operations that threatened to end his career.

"There came a point," Richie reveals, "when I was doubting my ability to survive, times when I was very depressed, totally out of it."

The self-professed "humaholic," planned to cool his jets for just a year, "which was my plan, but then life took over," he says, when his father, a retired army captain whom he adored, became ill and died at age seventy-five in October 1990: "Did you say cry?" the singer whispers. "The word is *unglued*—it was the most unsettling

thing I had ever experienced. Dad was my rock."

Simultaneously, Richie was diagnosed in 1988 with polyps on one of his vocal cords, requiring three surgeries over three years: "That scared the absolute death out of me, man. To me, it was open heart surgery, because my vocal chords were *everything* to me, and my doctor said it was possible I would never sing again."

Moreover, Richie says his "inner life was falling to pieces totally," when his marriage crashed, most dramatically in 1988. Brenda Richie, desperate to have a baby and tortured for years by her husband's roving eye, finally erupted into a violent temper tantrum at two A.M. on June 29, 1988. She tracked down Richie kissing good night a twenty-two-year-old model-dancer named Diane Alexander.

"It was the argument of life talking out loud," says Richie. Brenda, screaming obscenities, kicked Richie violently in the stomach or groin—reports vary— next attacking Alexander. Left behind was a trail of blood, hair, and broken glass. "Two words," Richie says of his feelings that night, "anger and humiliation," brought on by years of "procrastination," he says, neglecting the needs

of his wife. "That's called a great idea of escape. To do eleven years on the road and say I was pure . . . of course not. I had the latest and greatest affairs of life. I call that being very human."

Although the marriage is kaput and Richie's voice is totally healed, his world is still upside down: "Where am I?" he asks plaintively. "Am I capable of doing the right thing in a relationship? How much of this was my fault? What did I do wrong?

"The tests of life taught me I could *survive* real life," says the weathered star, now making a concert and recording comeback. "I'm a grown man now, and it's time to take flight again." But this is a new "flight machine"—one frayed and tempered by storms, no longer infallible: "Trying to be a hero was very difficult. I've learned I'm human, that I could survive. Now I'm a hero to myself."

# LIONEL RICHIE

# After a lifetime of impeccably

managing his wife Joan Rivers's career, Edgar Rosenberg lay in his Bel Air bedroom in the summer of 1987, staring at the ceiling, devastated by the abrupt cancellation of *The Late Show Starring Joan Rivers* in May.

"It wrecked my husband," says the comedienne, who passed through her bedroom puzzled by her husband's odd behavior. "He'd never lie down in the middle of the day," Rivers remembers. "I should have seen the signs, his suddenly putting all his affairs in tiptop order, but I was so terribly depressed myself."

Weakened by a 1984 heart attack, gout, a hiatus hernia, and high blood pressure, Rosenberg was found dead at sixty-two in a Philadelphia hotel room after taking an overdose of Valium on August 14, 1987.

Joan read the suicide note two days later at home: "Of course, he told me he loved me," she remembers, tears filling her eyes, "but that I was better off without him."

Rivers ravaged Rosenberg's medicine chest and smashed dozens of bottles against the bathroom floor. "You son of a bitch!" she howled. "Two thirds of my life were gone—my career and my hus-

band. But I still had Melissa," the couple's daughter.

Melissa suggested a healing cruise to Greece, which they took. "We felt suspended in time, like floating in a balloon. We talked, cried, laughed, and got over the shock."

When the trip ended, Rivers's renaissance began. "I had led a tremendously sheltered life. Edgar did literally everything else for me—the bills, the contracts. I didn't know where the outside light switches were to the house.

"The turning point was waking up and growing up. I had to become a big girl and put my life back together again by myself."

And she did. Rivers began therapy and moved to New York, battling back, first on *Hollywood Squares*, then on Broadway in Neil Simon's *Broadway Bound*, and now on *The Joan Rivers Show* in between promoting The Joan Rivers Jewelry Collection on the QVC Network.

Serene and sleek and brimming with jokes, Rivers is filled with optimism. But, she says, "I still don't believe it. I miss Edgar . . . still drive past my house, which I've sold, and I still want to drive up that driveway because I know Edgar's going to come out the door. . . . You *never* believe it. But I

had to start believing it, and thank God, I'm feeling strong."

# JOAN RIVERS

# The tap-dancing, slapsticking

dervish made his burlesque debut at the age of fifteen months, appearing as a midget equipped with a tuxedo and a big rubber cigar. By 1939, Mickey Rooney, just nineteen, was MGM's top-grossing star—a shockingly immature genius who would watch his stardom fade alongside seven disastrous marriages.

"That immaturity was the paradox of a child who was a man, and a man who tried to remain a child," says a wizened Rooney, who recently bared all in his best-selling autobiography, *Life Is Too Short*.

"I've never been ashamed of marrying eight times," pouts the diminutive Brooklyn-born star, bluntly ticking off his melodramatic, sometimes comic marital mishaps.

Wife number one, Ava Gardner: "Bottom line, we didn't have God in our home. There was no room for intimacy, no room for being a human being."

He proposed to wife number two, Alabama beauty queen Betty Jane Rase, "right after the seventeenth bourbon," he recalls. "When I got sober, she got too tall, an Amazon—I came up to her navel."

Wife number three, Martha Vickers, cited Rooney's temper and infidelities in divorce court. Rooney responds: "I had a short fuse. Who

wouldn't? She was drinking a quart of Scotch a day and smelled like a distillery."

Next came Elaine Mahnken, who was driven crazy by Rooney's gambling at the track. "Nobody ever mentioned she was seeing somebody else. My heart was broken."

Rooney's next wife, Barbara Thomason, was also unfaithful. "She had taken a lover who murdered her in 1966, shot her in the face with my thirty-eight, then put a bullet in his own brain. He might just as well have put one in mine. It killed me, pal. You don't want to see Mickey Rooney weighing one hundred six pounds." Two more disastrous marriages, to Margie Lane for one year and Carolyn Hockett for five, followed.

Meanwhile, Rooney's career collapsed into bankruptcy, mired in his addiction to barbiturates: "My god, it's the old song—tired of living, afraid of dying. I couldn't sleep, my brain was fried. I was suicidal, weak like putty."

Salvation finally intervened at Lake Tahoe in 1968. "I was eating my lunch when a busboy with golden, gossamer, almost ethereal hair came over to the table. He said, 'I was sent here to tell you that Jesus Christ loves you very much.' Then he turned and walked away.

It was a visitation by an angel. That was the turning point in my life— thereafter giving my life to Christ and becoming a newborn Christian. I went down on my knees, knew I had to go home to my Father."

And so he did. Solvency came with *Sugar Babies* in 1979, and his eighth marriage, to Jan Chamberlin, is "alive and ticking after seventeen years," he says. Rooney, the father of eleven, grandfather of four, is also a born-again author. The secret of success on the eighth try? "Believing in God, letting him run our home and our lives."

Rooney insists on leaving advice for anybody hooked on a drug or a bad marriage: "Turn to God and give your troubles to him. If I can make it, anyone can make it, because I was hooked, baby. Now, my Lord has fixed it so that my cup runneth over."

# MICKEY ROONEY

# Little Johnny was transported

to Hollywood, New York, Paris, and Madrid, savoring bullfights with Pablo Picasso, dinner with Igor Stravinsky and finger-painting with playmates Liza Minnelli and Candice Bergen.

"I was the baby of the family, extremely adaptable, treated as a *junior adult*," recalls the actor John Rubinstein, now carving out a directing career in New York as he fields acting parts, too.

Today his own man, the actor once withered in the shadow of his legendary father, pianist Arthur Rubinstein, who turned sixty the year Johnny was born. "He was an atypical, intimidating father—older than any dad on the block, European, and very formal," Rubinstein recalls. "I could never imagine telling him to shut up. He was the CEO and I was a private. Kids were subordinate human beings."

All this led, Rubinstein says, to "an underdeveloped muscle of self-esteem. The music of *me*— exactly who I was—got lost. I was a light bulb and he was a spotlight."

Light-bulb Johnny started piano practice at age four: "I had a great ear and a very deep understanding of music, but I was never going to be a virtuoso. My dad's 'prognosis-diagnosis' was that I should be a conductor. When I

started leaning toward my other hero—Fred Astaire—and loving show music, Dad considered me a traitor," though the elder Rubinstein eventually relented, proud of his son's five film scores and his 1980 Tony for *Children of a Lesser God*.

In later years, when his father lost his vision and suffered from colon cancer, Rubinstein says he started to notice a profound change in himself: "Yes, a very slow, gradual realization that I had made myself *secondary* to conform to Dad's life. Parts of me were put on hold, parts that needed to breathe. Instead of driving and pushing, I slowly discovered in myself an ability to stand and enjoy."

Breathing also included "great upheavals" in the actor's life, including a divorce from his wife of nineteen years. "It's a personal refocusing that goes beyond a mid-life crisis," he reasons obliquely, refusing to discuss the collapse of his marriage. "Now I'm happier, less anxious, more interested in things in the world, less selfish. I could always be the son of Arthur Rubinstein when he was alive, but I can't hide behind that anymore."

When the great Rubinstein died in 1982, at age ninety-five, his youngest son was at last free to be himself. "The weird thing about

Dad's death—and it's a difficult thing to confess," he says, "is that I don't miss him very much and don't think I ever did. But I do miss his *music*. When I listen to it, I experience a very, very deep baby-Daddy feeling for my father. I feel him *talking* to me more profoundly and intimately than he did in person."

# JOHN RUBINSTEIN

# Love struck so suddenly.

There she was, at eight P.M., a single woman preparing to host *Saturday Night Live*. By midnight, she was hungrily kissing the show's dashing executive producer.

"And six weeks later, I married him," beams Susan Saint James, remembering the red-letter night in 1980 when she met NBC honcho producer Dick Ebersol. (Ebersol, you'll recall, got the blame for replacing *Today*'s Jane Pauley with Deborah Norville, apparently triggering the program's ratings slide.)

"I got married in a sorta haze," says the then-Hollywood-based actress. She was happily pregnant by the following spring, her bicoastal life an idyllic one until "the fall day of 1981 when Harmony [her son by prior marriage], then eight, was hit by a car."

Saint James grimaces. "He was playing on a nearby movie lot, a car came out of nowhere, and his femur was broken in half. He was put into traction for six weeks," a momentous gestation period for the entire family.

"At first, I was *so cool*. I told Dick he didn't need to come to L.A. But when I called my dad, I completely fell apart. There I was pregnant, my son in the hospital, my husband living in New York—this was not going to work. I asked

myself: 'Why did I get married? I'm still a single parent and I hate it.'

"Suddenly, I knew either the marriage was going to fail, or I was going to have to move. Two days after Harm was out of the hospital, I told my secretary: 'Pack it up and send it east—twenty thousand pounds of stuff. I'm not afraid to make big decisions.'

"Being willing to make a change by moving east really solidified the commitment," says Saint James, now a full-time mother to older children Sunshine, Harmony, and the little Ebersols—Charlie and William and the baby, Teddy.

Playing Mama Saint James in northwestern Connecticut, and tuckered out from five years of *Kate & Allie*, the stunning actress declares herself retired from show biz, though she's active as president of the state's Special Olympics group and spokeswoman for the Diet Center Program.

"And I'm so happy I'm not acting. After twenty-three years, I'm phasing totally out and over. Phase one," she smiles, "was getting to be a famous TV star; phase two was my dream to marry a dashing man, have an elegant lifestyle, and raise my children."

Phase three? "A business career. I'm thinking of buying our

local FM radio station, creating my own perfume, clothing—and I'm collating research for a book about my life."

"I'm not afraid," she says, "of adding another child, being another person, being a new thing. I like taking risks!"

# SUSAN SAINT JAMES

201

# In this true-to-life fairy

tale, the Prince of Fortune kisses a German Sleeping Beauty, and, within a blink, the attractive blonde awakens and becomes the grandest model of them all—Amazon-tall, rich, and famous.

"And now my passport is a wreck," smiles super-Fräulein Claudia Schiffer, the twenty-one-year-old cover girl just back from Africa, the French Antilles, Australia, Thailand, and Morocco. She'll go anywhere for a $50,000-per-photo shoot.

Not bad for the daughter of a small-town lawyer in Rheinberg, Germany—the oldest of four—who dreamed of becoming a lawyer, just like Dad.

"I was a very shy, very good German girl," she says demurely, "the tallest in my class," a German giraffe sprouting to six feet in her mid-teens, and bearing a startling resemblance to the young Brigitte Bardot. "Some boys," she giggles, "went crazy over me, but I wasn't a vain girl and my mother never told me I was beautiful."

That all changed the fateful night sixteen-year-old Claudia drove with friends from Rheinberg to Düsseldorf for a night of disco-ing at the popular "Checkers" nightclub. "We were dancing and having a lot of fun when"—she pauses, smiling—"it happened,"

the appearance of Michel Levatton, owner of a French modeling agency named Metropolitan.

"This stranger came up to me and said: 'I'm going to make you a model.' I thought: 'Oh, sure, maybe modeling underwear in your apart-ment.' I just laughed him off. But he was persistent and kept follow-ing me around. Finally, I told him he could call my parents."

The Schiffers soon agreed to send Claudia off to Paris to do test shots. "I was sure I'd be sent back to Germany fast once Michel saw the photos, but I was very, very sur-prised by what I saw. With make-up, I looked older—really good."

To say the least. Little Miss Schiffer debuted at the top, on the cover of French *Elle*—"I was smil-ing on every newspaper kiosk in Paris," she beams—and since then she has done roughly a hundred magazine covers, earning her more than $1 million per year.

Schiffer, who in a recent, widely seen gig as the model for Guess Jeans appeared barely dressed in scooped-out necklines, wearing mostly facial expressions of sexual ecstasy, is asked what happened to that nice young girl who wanted to become a lawyer? Who is that woman in those pictures? "That's not me, definitely not," she insists. "When I put on the makeup, the

bikini, the false eyelashes, I get into the mood and become a different person. I'm acting; I enjoy being 'the other woman'—but it's not me."

But Schiffer has been changed by her experience. "Sure, I'm much more secure and confi-dent, more mature. And I've become more suspicious about men. I have one boyfriend," she confides, a six-foot-four-inch model, "and one is enough."

The biggest lesson of all for the world's most sought-after body and face? "The look on your face doesn't mean anything. When you open your mouth, that's what's real."

# CLAUDIA SCHIFFER

203

# "Daaaaling, don't be a fool,

call the man!" scolded Zsa Zsa Gabor.

The Daaaaling, an aspiring actress named Jorja Curtright, had just met Zsa Zsa's friend Sidney, a hotshot scriptwriter courting anything in a skirt with a pulse.

"Why shouldn't I have been?" grins bestselling novelist Sidney Sheldon, savoring a look back before literary stardom hit."Right after I saw Jorja," Sheldon remembers, I said: 'I just met the woman I'm going to marry.' Just looking at her, talking for a minute, I *knew*."

Jorja minded her Hungarian matchmaker, phoned Sheldon, and six months later the couple married. The next thirty-four years were filled with daughter Mary and constant traipsing around the world. "Also, because Jorja was such a good actress, she was also a wonderful editor," says Sheldon. "She could always catch a false line." But in December 1985, she complained of deadening fatigue.

"I took her to the doctor, and as she walked into his office she literally keeled over of a heart attack, went into intensive care, and was gone two days later. It was a stunning, complete shock. . . . Thank God she didn't suffer."

Two weeks later, Sheldon— the author of 250 television scripts,

eight Broadway plays, thirty motion pictures, and ten novels— sat sobbing as he wrote the key scene in *Windmills of the Gods*, in which the heroine's husband is killed in a car crash: "*Nothing was going to be all right again. Ever. Goodbye, my darling. Death is supposed to be an ending, but for me it was the beginning of an unbearable hell. I don't want to live.*"

"I felt exactly that way," Sheldon whispers.

Until four years ago, when the novelist walked into a dinner party and spotted a young divorcée. The love lightning struck again.

"I didn't even *talk* to Alexandra that night: I just looked at her and suddenly *knew*—again. It was much deeper than something physical: It's an aura." The couple married in 1989.

"This isn't a happy ending . . . but a beginning," says the seventy-five-year-old, who insists the twenty-five-year difference in age between himself and leggy blond Alexandra Kosoff, once a child actress, means nothing: "Love crosses those superficial boundaries easily," he says.

"Alexandra and I will be together until the day we die. . . . I never thought I'd be lucky enough to say that again!"

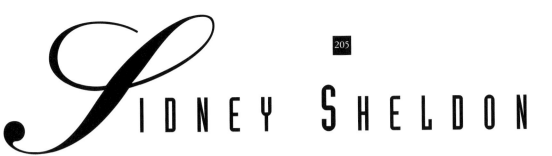

# SIDNEY SHELDON

# Once upon a time, two German

boys, small-town dreamers, craved adventure on the high seas. Coincidentally, both wound up working aboard the luxury cruise ship *Bremen*.

Magic was about to occur. The platinum blond from Rosenheim, named Siegfried Fischbacher, was the ship's star bartender, and also wowed the ladies with his solo magic act.

The dark-haired Roy Ludwig Van Horn—an animal lover from Bremerhaven who traveled with a pet cheetah—worked as a steward, hoping for a career in the hotel business.

"I watched Siegfried's act every night," Roy remembers, "and finally asked him if he could use my cheetah instead of his rabbit."

"At first, I didn't know what he was talking about," Siegfried recalls, though soon enough the blond magician had found himself a partner.

"The relationship," Siegfried remembers, "grew slowly. Roy was more the illusionist-dreamer, very positive; I was always more realistic, practical-minded and negative. Sometimes he could be too sure, so I brought him down, and he lifted me up and we met in the middle. And that's what made Siegfried and Roy tick."

Did it ever. After two years aboard the *Bremen*, the illusionists hit solid ground in 1968. A month later, they grabbed an invitation to perform at a gala for Princess Grace . . . and the rest is history.

"That meeting twenty-five years ago was the turning point of our lives," Siegfried believes, astounded even today by Roy's prowess with animals.

The Siegfried-Roy menagerie of twenty-eight exotic creatures includes the nearly extinct blue-eyed white tiger. "There are just under a hundred of them left in the world," says Roy, a fierce preservationist, "and we have eighteen of them," including the world's only snow-white male, who floats in midair across the stage, all six hundred pounds of him.

You can catch him and the rest of Siegfried and Roy's $25 million space-age stage show—complete with a cast of seventy—at the Mirage Hotel in Las Vegas, where the illusionists reign as the city's top tourist attraction, charging nearly a hundred dollars a ticket, and sitting on a long-term contract worth $57.5 million.

Do they ever wonder what would have happened if they hadn't met?

"That question doesn't exist," Roy declares. "It was meant to be."

"I don't believe in coincidence," sighs Siegfried. "It had to be . . . for sure . . . and I like happy endings."

# SIEGFRIED & ROY

# At ten a.m., a tall,

red-haired woman, posture-perfect, slowly makes her way down a pristine beach adjacent to her Martha's Vineyard summer house, alone, pondering what comes next in her life.

Wearing no makeup, no ball gown, not even humming, she is recognized anyway by a pretzel salesman offering his salty wares. She shakes her head, "No, thank you."

"Thank *you*, Miss Sills," he says in parting.

Who can forget the shimmering soprano and mischievous red curls of America's opera sweetheart, Beverly Sills, who retired from the stage in 1980, only to face another crossroads in 1989.

After a decade of funneling her powerhouse temperament into balancing budgets and soothing unions as chieftain of the New York City Opera, she left the company and the world of classical music.

After that, she said, "I began facing a whole new world of decisions about what I would like to do.

"I didn't want to make up my mind right away," though adjusting to a no-work routine was painful, she recalled. "Ohhhh. I couldn't sleep and my husband (businessman Peter Greenough) said I should just lie there, not move, even if I was wide-awake."

No matter what her next job, anything would be easier, she laughs, than dealing with singers: "I never knew how easy it was to take care of one pair of vocal cords. At City Opera, I had two hundred pairs of vocal cords! I was their mother. When I was an opera star, I never spent sixteen hours a day singing. That was much more glamorous."

Would Sills like to perform yet again? "I don't miss the pressure, but I miss singing. Right now I've got to make some big decisions."

Although hosting a TV talk show, managing a record company, and running a publishing house were all under consideration, Sills has taken no job in the last three years, instead focusing her energies on taking care of her elderly mother, Shirley, and tending to daughter, Muffy, and husband, Peter, who suffers from arthritis. She also sits on dozens of boards and relishes speaking engagements and the occasional hosting of an arts-related event.

Meanwhile, she has savored a cruise up the Nile, fishing in New Zealand, and sunning in Mexico. Guilty?

"I deserve it," she says. "I've been a slave to work and I'm certainly never ever going to take a job that begins at 7:45 A.M. with no cap at the other end of the day."

Stay tuned.

# BEVERLY SILLS

# The school blimp was

everybody's last choice for a friend.

"In eighth grade I weighed two hundred pounds and stood only four feet nine inches!" grimaces health and fitness guru Richard Simmons—ex-member of what he calls the "fried generation." "Everything in my house was fried. When I saw my first fish in an aquarium, I asked my mother: 'Where's the crust?'"

By age ten, the plump boy with the court-jesting humor was miserable: "Food was my mistress—my only friend. In high school, I was beaten up, mocked. It was totally traumatic—devastating to my self-esteem. I was supposedly *bad* because I was fat."

To console himself, the boy would eat even more. A typical breakfast was French toast and pancakes, four fried eggs, a half pound of bacon, and two big glasses of juice.

"It was culinary suicide," says Simmons, who sprouted to five-feet-six by his eighteenth birthday, with his weight hovering at 268 pounds, his waist at forty-eight inches. A year later, disheartened by the failure of endless crash diets and fads, Simmons at nineteen starved himself down to an anorexic 122 pounds. His motivation, he says, was an unsigned note attached to the windshield of his car at college.

"The note read: 'Dear Richard: You're very funny, but fat people die young. Please don't die.'

"*That* was my turning point. I almost died from starving myself down to a twenty-inch waist after that. Then, after recovering in the hospital from dehydration, I buried myself in a New Orleans library, learning the basic food groups, reading nutrition books, trying to find a diet that would work for me. I came up with a 1,400-to 1,600-calorie plan per day."

He took it to Los Angeles in 1973: "I tried to join a gym but felt like an ugly duckling next to those buffed-up guys with muscles. When I saw a 240-pound woman turned away at a health club—she was 'too fat and sloppy'—I started my own exercise studio: Slimmons. That was sixteen years ago."

Now skinny—155 pounds, he claims—and rich, the talk show maven swears by videos like his *Sweatin' to the Oldies*, while continuing to slim the unconverted with his "Salad Sprays" and "Deal-A-Meal" diet regimen, all heavily promoted on cable television.

"Our society believes fat people are bad, stupid, lazy, sluggish, undependable, and too emotional," he says.

"Wrong. There are no scales at the gates of heaven—but living on this earth in a body you hate is no good—and thanks to the right diet and exercise, it's not necessary."

# RICHARD SIMMONS

# The private terror began early.

On the day Carly Simon was born, she nearly died.

"The doctor asked my father: 'Shall I save your wife or your child?' My father said: 'Save my wife.' I just happened to live by a stroke of good obstetrics.

"I was a placenta previa *and* a breech birth," explains Carly, pointing to one possible reason for "a very delicate nervous system" that has left her one of the pop world's most stage-shy performers.

As "a very shy, anxious" child, Carly plowed ahead with show biz, despite what she terms "a crippling, embarrassing stammer and a stutter, too."

Throughout the seventies, Simon bravely attempted public performances, but in 1981 she collapsed at a concert in Pittsburgh, paralyzed by heart palpitations. At the time, she was stressed out by both her crumbling marriage to singer James Taylor and her son Ben's illness, which forced him to have a kidney removed. She lost twenty-five pounds.

"I was in terrible shape physically and emotionally," Simon remembers. "You could call it a nervous breakdown." Seven difficult years followed, in which both her personal life and career deteriorated.

"I basically couldn't get arrested," she recalls, sadly. "I lost two record contracts in quick succession," and, more important, "I lost my self-esteem . . . I lost myself."

Consoling herself by writing music, Simon emerged from her cocoon in 1987, first singing for an audience of three hundred in a concert on Martha's Vineyard, then penning "Coming Around Again," the theme song for Mike Nichols's film *Heartburn*. Voilà: the first Carly hit in seven years. At the end of that year, she married poet Jim Hart.

She's been on fire ever since. In 1989 she won an Oscar, a Grammy, and a Golden Globe for the theme song for the movie *Working Girl*. Her collection of smoldering standards, *My Romance*, sold over four hundred thousand copies and has been followed by even more hits.

"My confidence has improved, I trust my instincts much more, and I no longer see myself as being terribly fragile. Still, I haven't conquered the problem of stage fright, and I have no answers.

"One doctor," she says, "said it was an inner ear problem—that I get dizzy from the stage lights and audience noise. I don't know what it is anymore," nor does it matter, she says.

"It's my lot in life," shrugs Simon, otherwise reveling in her new happy marriage and children, Sally and Ben. "I'm a homebody and would never tour again—it's not worth it to me. I love recording, I love writing, and I love being with my children.

"I've learned that nobody's perfect," Simon says, "and I don't *expect* myself to be perfect anymore. I don't want to perform in Yankee Stadium anyway."

# CARLY SIMON

# The Texas girl—a ballet

fanatic with an overactive conscience—was entranced by her maternal grandfather, a Methodist minister who preached the gospel in her hometown of Houston until he died in 1976 at age 102.

"My Paw-Paw was the strongest influence in my life," declares actress Jaclyn Smith who remembers him as "a totally *fair* human being—a man neither black nor white, but with some gray in him."

Yet on the subject of premarital sex, Paw-Paw drew the line.

"You *didn't* have sex with a man unless you married him, and because of my upbringing, I married when I shouldn't have. Three times."

She first married actor Roger Davis, in 1969. "It *wasn't* even a marriage," snaps the actress, apparently still bitter.

The lies of romance, she says, still smart: "I was innocent, very naive, and not prepared for a careless man who wasn't faithful. It was shocking to me." Smith sued for divorce in 1974.

Next, at the height of her fame as one of "Charlie's Angels" in 1977, Smith married husband number two, football jock-turned-actor Dennis Cole. It lasted three years. "He was a stabilizing force back then, but my being on a hit

show did his ego as an actor no good. He resented my fame. I divorced him. And as I look back, neither marriage was 'real'—there was no commitment, no sense of family—and I view both marriages as total failures."

Then, while filming *Nightkill* in 1980, Smith became infatuated with British cinematographer Tony Richmond: "I saw this man literally paint with light—and I liked his looks the minute I saw him." She married Richmond the following year.

"Tony changed my life. We were a team, he thought of me before himself, and we had two beautiful children," Gaston and Spencer. "He also took joy in my career. No competition."

Yet after seven years, Smith says, Richmond's alcoholism played havoc with their marriage. And he sued her for divorce in 1989.

"I don't drink, I don't smoke, and I've never touched a drug," she says. "That's the Devil. Tony's drinking was a continuing problem. He'd cover it up; then I'd feel betrayed. The divorce is pending.

"It's crazy, because I was the girl who dreamed of marrying just once, but it hasn't happened," Smith exclaims. "Why? It's sad, but I've learned that when a marriage fails, your life isn't over."

"My life," she smiles, "is great. I marvel at the joy of my two children. And yeah, I have three marriages that failed, but it hasn't made me cynical. I'm still a romantic."

Marriage a fourth time?

"Oh, sure," she says, "but not right away. I have to sew myself up first. I don't want another failure. When you're a romantic, wedding bells are always ringing, and the fairy-tale wedding is not always the solution."

# JACLYN SMITH

# The blond-haired girl,

terrified of her drunk dad, huddled in a dark closet, convinced she might be killed. "Night after night, my heart was pounding until I was finally pushed to the breaking point," remembers sitcom star Suzanne Somers. Today she's buoyant on television again and in her "infomercial" success with the new, notorious Thighmaster. She's also a frequent lecturer to children of alcoholics.

For the actress, who helped establish the Suzanne Somers Institute for the Effects of Addictions on the Family, life began in San Bruno, California, with the Mahoney kids—Dan, Michael, Maureen, and Suzanne—all of them terrorized by their father, Frank: "He was the tyrant and we were the slaves," Somers remembers. "It was total chaos. Total insanity. Constant raging and fighting and screaming and swearing."

The stressed girl wet her bed regularly until age twelve: "Humiliating, and my father made fun of me for it!" she says. By seventeen the volcano erupted: "When he ripped my prom dress off me, told me I was 'nothin',' I slammed him in the head with a tennis racket until his blood spurted like a fountain."

To escape this house of horror, Suzanne became pregnant at age seventeen in 1965. She married the infant's father, Bruce Somers: "Getting pregnant and getting a divorce a year later only contributed to my low self-esteem and need for constant crises."

Indeed, the actress was arrested for check fraud, her car was impounded, and she secretly had an abortion after embarking on an affair with a married man—TV host Allen Hamel, whom she would later marry: "Back then I was lying, manipulating, hiding, and frightened to death," she says. "I blamed myself for *everything*, thought I was mentally retarded."

Then, in 1971, her six-year-old son, Bruce Jr., was run over by a car: Although the boy made a complete physical recovery, "Bruce," she says, "had terrible nightmares and nightsweats for months afterward. I finally took him to a psychiatrist." Her son's treatment led to her own. "That was *my* turning point," three intensive years of gut-wrenching therapy that led to her 1988 bestselling book, *Keeping Secrets*. "I sobbed every single day I wrote the book, forgiving myself, forgiving my father. Bruce's accident was a gift that allowed me to learn the greatest lesson in life: that I had value, that my father's disease was not my disease, that I could

choose to be a victim or take hold of my life."

The actress, now nearly fifty, and still happily married to manager Hamel, recently wrote *Wednesday's Children*, a book of celebrity triumphs over abuse. "Wednesday's child," she says in parting, "is full of woe, but a child who also survives and forgives."

# SUZANNE SOMERS

# By the time seven gold medals

had been strung around Mark Spitz's neck at the 1972 Olympics in Munich, the twenty-one-year-old swimmer had churned out 26,000 miles of butterfly strokes in preparation. His athletic prowess and endurance earned him $5 million in endorsements that lucky year—and even a little media overexposure.

Then, he traded in his red, white, and blue Speedo for a business suit and a Ferrari, and subsequently anchored ABC sports events, plunking his endorsement cash into L.A. real estate.

Next, in 1990, Spitz, then forty, decided to attempt the near impossible. He wanted to win a shot at the gold in the 1992 Olympic Games in Barcelona.

"A writer friend dared me to try, and I began to wonder what would happen if I swam four hours a day, plus weight training. I was *curious* to see if somebody my age could swim the hundred-meter butterfly."

Just what had he been doing to keep fit over the years? "To be honest," he grins, "not much of anything. For nineteen years, I felt like skippin' workout and had such a thrill out of that, you can't imagine!"

Starting was therefore painful. "At first, I was terrible and I could barely survive the workout,"

he groans. "I had to get used to pain. But my body really snapped back and my weight dropped from 194 to 175." Unluckily, Spitz ruptured a disc just three months before his first comeback event, the Clairol Option Challenge swim meet in April 1991.

"Because of the disc problem, I wasn't able to practice my starts until thirty days before the race, which wasn't enough time," he explains. He forged ahead anyway, bravely competing against current Olympic superstars Tom Jager and Matt Biondi. Terrorized by pressure and the press, handicapped by his back and slow starts, the former Olympian lost both races. "I'm just a human being," Spitz says shrugging, "and I'm bound to make a few mistakes. I lost them right at the start. I basically fell apart, started scrambling my stroke." That meant he took twenty-four strokes across the pool instead of his normal twenty. His final time was 26.70 seconds versus Jager's 24.92. Though less than two seconds behind, in swimming, where hundredths of seconds separate winners from also-rans, his finish looked dismal.

When the race ended, Spitz was not depressed. "Nope. Relieved. It was inevitable I was probably going to lose, though I

never wanted to admit it. I'm not using my age as an excuse, but after being away eighteen-and-a-half years, how could I expect myself to control all my nerves? Losing by just literally one stroke wasn't bad!"

Cheered on by Suzy, his wife of nineteen years, and by his ten-year-old son, Matthew Eric, Spitz remained determined to make the Olympic team, though he ultimately failed to do so. He has pulled out of the water an important lesson for himself and his son: "If you want to pursue a dream, there's nothing like the present. For my son, my losing was very humbling; it's good for him to learn about not only winning but losing, too—to know it's okay for daddy to lose."

# MARK SPITZ

219

# Agony, right from the start.

Crammed into a stifling, hot charity ward on the lower East Side, the infant's mother wailed as a frenzied physician delivered the baby, Michael Sylvester Stallone, with forceps—and severed the infant's facial nerve on the left side. A botched birth, July 6, 1942.

"Half my tongue, lip, and chin were paralyzed, so sometimes it's very hard to ar-ti-cu-late," says megahero Sylvester Stallone, smiling. Once a skinny kid with rickets, he never pictured himself as a movie star.

After all, the oddball with a speech impediment, lopsided mouth, and droopy eyes was tormented by neighborhood punks in Hell's Kitchen. They called him Sylvia.

"I was like Mr. Potato Head with all the parts in the wrong places," he says, laughing, "and wanted to be anybody but me."

Seething with "the murderous rage of retaliation," he recalls, the boy would swat flies off cars with a lead pipe. Then he got whipped by his "rough, very rough" father until he bled. "Dad said, 'You weren't born with much of a brain, so you'd better develop your body.'"

Finding "salvation" in bodybuilding as a teen, the tortured youth coached soccer at an American college in Leysin, Switzerland, in 1964, where he discovered acting—"something not illegal and yet soul-satisfying."

Later, after dropping out of the University of Miami drama school, he struggled in New York, ushering at a movie theater and sweeping out Bronx Zoo lion cages in between reading about screenwriting and begging for bit parts.

"Swallowing criticism and rejection and despair and still being vulnerable as an actor is tough," Stallone explains. "I steeled myself against the terrible, terrible, terrible onslaught of rejection: 'You're no good, you're too short, you're stupid.'"

Hungry for success? "No. *Starving.* You have to be." And then, as the now-legendary story goes, with only $106 in his bank account, Stallone dictated the script of *Rocky* to his then-pregnant wife, Sasha, in three-and-half days.

Turning down $265,000 for the script that would not have used him in the starring role, he instead accepted $75,000 plus 10 percent of the net profits. *Rocky*, released in 1976, was nominated for two Oscars and earned $250 million. The rest—the $30 million salary per picture, the $1 billion-plus in box-office gross for the slew of *Rocky, Rambo*, and other films that followed—is history.

Fate, destiny, hard work, or dumb luck? "Hard work and talent. I just knew what I wanted. It had nothing to do with looks or muscle." What then? "Essence. There are guys more muscular with prettier faces and they're not in the movies."

If Stallone's essence had a name, what would it be? "Mmm. Soul. Just soul: an eternal internal fire. Pain stokes it, and fear brings it to the surface."

# SYLVESTER STALLONE

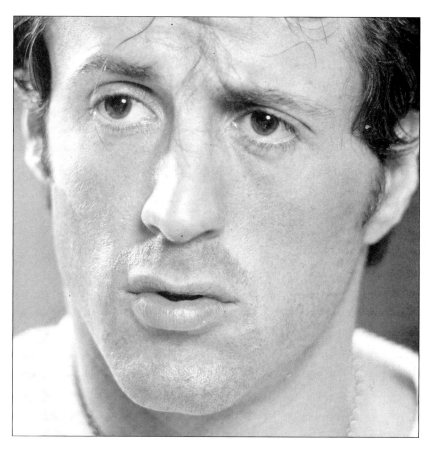

# Picture this: Elizabeth

Taylor enters a room rubbing sesame oil into her skin. Arms opening wide, violet eyes flashing, she invites you to come closer: "Feel me . . . my arms, my neck. That's right, my face, too."

It happened to me, I did, and I can tell you the oil must work. She chuckles, looks into the mirror, then says she sees "something that needs to be fixed, dear."

Vibrant and set to launch into making theatrical films once again, the mature Taylor turns the conversation serious these days, for she remains haunted by the turning point—the 1985 death of her friend Rock Hudson—which prompted her to singlehandedly raise $40 million as chairperson of AMFAR (American Foundation for AIDS Research). She has also established The (patient-care oriented) Elizabeth Taylor AIDS Foundation.

"Rock," she begins simply, "was my sweetest friend, and I miss him terribly."

A favorite memory?

"Oh yes," she smiles hazily, thinking back to the set of *Giant* in 1955: "Walking in a summer storm in Texas, collecting hailstones the size of golf balls, and putting them in our Bloody Marys!"

Her worst memory was a visit to Hudson a few days before his death: "I've never seen a more painful, cruel, degrading death," she whispers, now close to tears. "When I saw Rock the day before he died, he didn't know me—he had no idea where he was. So lonely. The brain, mercifully, seems to totally disintegrate."

And there has been little peace for Taylor since: "I'm god-damned sick and tired of people blaming gay men for AIDS. It was an *accident* that the disease was picked up by homosexuals in Haiti. It could just as easily have been spread by some horny rich babe from Miami.

"African men and women probably got it from eating the verdant monkey, who happens to be an adorable creature, but deadly. So if people are going to put the blame anywhere—why don't they just blame the *goddamned* green monkey?"

"AIDS," Elizabeth shouts, violet eyes now flashing, "is *not* a sin, it's a disease—and the insanity of homophobia has got to stop. I'm wiped out every time I hear about people who still think you can get the AIDS virus through the air, through sweat glands or tears.

"The government has cold scientific knowledge, but I don't think it's heard about AIDS from an emotional heterosexual woman like me. I'm not an endangered species—although I've had blood transfusions, so maybe I am. We're all potential victims, for Christ's sake." She grits her teeth. "But people just think: 'Well, babies got it from the sins of their mothers, or an adult got it accidentally from a transfusion—so they're not as guilty as the homosexuals.' That's bullshit. Everybody's an innocent victim. It's a hit-and-miss deadly bullet."

Not to be stopped, Taylor leaves me with these words: "Whatever happened to compassion? And to caring? What happened to the Ten Commandments? How dare so-called religious people say it was God's idea, His wrath to kill the homosexuals. We're all God's children."

# ELIZABETH TAYLOR

# Perched high in his home in

the Hollywood Hills, staring down three stories onto his back lawn to keep an eye on his three triplet daughters, Richard Thomas nine years ago was living in a world growing fainter, though he didn't know it.

"I couldn't hear the girls too clearly . . . no consonants, no high vowels, though I could see their lips moving," he would remember.

Two hours later, missing a chiming doorbell, he made tuna sandwiches for Barbara, Gwyneth, and Pilar. A ringing phone went unanswered.

That night, as he was savoring a Mahler Symphony on his stereo, the volume blaring, his wife, Alma, from whom he has now separated, entered the room with a family friend, Florence Pasquini, and emphatically turned the knob to off.

"You have a hearing problem," announced Florence, whose own husband suffered similarly, "and I'm going to take you to the best doctor in town." She meant Howard House, the audiologist who treated Ronald Reagan.

"Thank God, *take* him," Alma said, "because obviously something is wrong."

Three days later—"I was like a little lamb, never fought for a second the idea that I should go to a

doctor"—the then-thirty-two-year-old actor made famous by the TV series *The Waltons*, John Boy no longer, got the bad news.

"I had a fifty percent loss of hearing in *both* ears because of the deterioration of the auditory nerve—surprisingly common among men in their thirties," Thomas says. It is a neurological condition that could not be reversed, he was told.

He was given vitamin and mineral supplements to halt the deterioration of the nerve "and two hearing aids," state-of-the-art cosmetic dreams invisibly hidden in the actor's ear.

"Suddenly, on stage, instead of trying to counter a muffled perception of my voice—which had become tense and strained—I could hear it clearly and adjust it," says Thomas, now national chairman of the Better Hearing Institute.

Other pluses: "When I take them out, I sleep like a baby . . . and I can tune people I don't like right out by adjusting the volume."

However, now he has a different problem. "In the morning before I put them in, when I'm making breakfast for my kids, they have to repeat everything they tell me.

"Now they shout: 'DAD, WILL YOU PUT YOUR PLUGS IN. . .PLEASE!'"

# Harold Traywick from

Marshville, North Carolina, a farmer and a country music fanatic, wondered what to do with his hell-raising sons, Randy and Ricky. "Those boys," Traywick would later joke about the two eldest of his six kids, "got locked up in jail so much they'd take turns calling me. I must have bailed them out fifty times at two in the morning."

"We were a little wild," admits country star Randy Travis, flying high on a cross-country tour.

The little rebel was drawn to the bottle at age ten. "Dad wasn't around much, and when he was, he always drank—more and more as I got older. Then came peer pressure: 'Drink this, smoke this': Beer, liquor, wine, marijuana, acid, MDA, PHC, mushroom," all of it fueling his self-destruction: "After age thirteen," Travis continues, "I was hopeless." The out-of-control boy was arrested a number of times for DWI, public drunkenness, petty theft, and violating probation. "I totaled four vehicles at 135 miles per hour when I was fifteen, one motorcycle at eighty, and should have been dead by rights, period," he muses.

He bottomed out in 1977 at age seventeen, arrested for breaking into a convenience store and attempting to steal a pickup truck.

"Nobody could stop me," he says, until he walked into Lib Hatcher's nightclub, Country City, in Charlotte, North Carolina, and won a talent contest.

"That was the big turnaround of my life," he says with a smile. "Meeting Lib. I know for sure that I would have gone to prison for five years otherwise." But Hatcher, sixteen years older than Travis, intervened. "She told the judge I was working full-time for her, not drinking or using drugs," Travis says.

They fell in love. Hatcher left her husband of ten years, and the twosome moved to Nashville in 1982, where Travis was rejected by every label in town. "I painted houses, short-order-cooked catfish for three and a half years, washed dishes, and made demos." But in 1986, the swing back toward traditional country music merged with Travis's gift for cutting to the heart. His first effort, *Storms of Life*, sold three million albums and captured two Grammys and ten American Music Awards.

"I felt like I had hit the lottery," he says, though a shadow remained. "We were living together, unmarried; she was older, and Warner's advice was to deny the relationship."

Finally, in June 1991, after fourteen years together, the thirty-two-year-old singer married his forty-nine-year-old mentor, lover, and the couple reside on a one-hundred-acre farm in Tennessee crossed by paths marked Libby Lane and Travis Trails. He now earns about $10 million a year. And, he notes, "No drugs, cigarettes, or alcohol since I was nineteen!"

# RANDY TRAVIS

229

# In Wichita Falls, Texas,

servicing oil rigs paid the bills for the Tunes, but Tommy's brimming-with-talent father, Jim, was really a combination of country squire, Julia Child, and Fred Astaire.

"My dad," says Broadway kingpin Tommy, "was expert at training Tennessee walking horses, he was a magnificent cook, and, along with my mom, Eva, he was renowned in Texas for his ballroom dancing." No surprise then that the Tunes' son, Thomas James, practically danced out of the womb in 1939.

"In Texas," Tune explains, "there was a stigma about a boy dancing—guys joked about me at school—but at home my father wasn't the least embarrassed. Company would come over and he'd throw back the rug and make me strap on my tap shoes."

Springing from two parents he describes as "never tense, but balanced and levelheaded," the six-foot-six-and-a-half dancer spent the 1970s and 1980s dancing and choreographing his way to stardom in such Broadway hits as *Seesaw* (1973), *The Best Little Whorehouse in Texas* (1978), *Nine* (1982), and *Grand Hotel* (1990).

But during the same years, Tommy Tune also faced the darker side of life: "First, in 1975, my dad died of diverticulitis at age seventy-

five. My perception was that there had been a very thick cable that went from my solar plexus to Dad's. When he died, I was flipped and ripped in the middle. At first I didn't crack, but a year later, getting into a tux for an opening, I just broke, started weeping and weeping.

"I looked up and said: 'Dad, I hope you approve.' Suddenly, every-thing came together and I felt his strength entering me. That was the start of a turning point, a healing for me."

Such strength would be sore-ly needed in the eighties, when Tune lost a number of close friends to AIDS, including his mentor—famed choreographer Michael Bennett—and his agent of twenty-five years, ICM's Eric Shepard.

"I lost more people in the eighties than most people do in a lifetime," he says. "Nature is very unsentimental. If a blight falls on a beautiful tree, it's not the tree's fault. Life is a crapshoot. We're all dying."

His greatest blow, he says, was losing his mother, Eva, to can-cer in 1989: "Cancer was claiming her, but she was spunky—experi-encing the same slow dying that Otto Kringelein goes through in *Grand Hotel*."

Tune is a workaholic devoted to yoga: "I try to silence the chat-tering mind and bring peace to my

being, but I still feel like an orphan. I'm fifty-three, but if you reverse those two numbers and add them together, that's how old I feel.

"When I read a good review, my first impulse still is to clip it and send it to my mom. Then I say: 'Oops. There's nobody to send it to.'"

# Tommy Tune

# "Common sense is horse

sense," declares Dear Abby, ensconced in her sprawling Beverly Hills mansion, "and horse sense," she giggles, still girlish at seventy-two with that perennial hair-bob, "can be found in a stable mind."

Over the last thirty-three years, no two minds have dispensed more horse sense than the Friedman girls, identical twins Esther Pauline and Pauline Esther, "Eppie," and "Popo" of Sioux City, Iowa, reborn as Ann Landers and vying sister Dear Abby in 1956. It was a year when not only their names but their lives changed in ways neither could have predicted.

While Ann Landers inherited her mantle from the already-established Ann Landers column in Chicago, Abby, fiercely competitive, carved out her own territory in San Francisco, beginning on January 9, 1956.

But Ann *did* get a head start on Abby, no? "That," Abby snaps, "was a matter of four weeks. . . . She wasn't all that famous. . . . She took a name somebody else owned . . . while I created Dear Abby and owned my name right from the word *go*."

Not without risk. "My twin felt betrayed," confides Abby, "because I became syndicated. I insisted that the world was big enough for two good advice

columns and tried desperately to make her see it my way."

But nothing worked, and the twosome—who shared a crib and were married in a joint ceremony—hardly spoke for seven years in the early 1960s. Abby insists that competition with her sister was never a problem: "Not for me," she declares obliquely. "Oh, Lord, if one of us was hugely successful and the other trailing . . . but we are both enormously successful. What's the problem?"

Yet there was one. "At the time my coming on the scene was very painful for her," says Abby. But after thirty years still painful? "*So?* There I was, competition, which she did not plan on."

Although the twosome are chummy nowadays—"we read each other's columns every day and send Bravo! notes"—Abby wouldn't dream of turning to Ann for advice: "We're close, but no. This may sound very arrogant, but I never had a problem that forced me to seek . . . professional help. I handle aggravation and irritation on my own or talk to my husband," millionaire businessman Mort Phillip, hitched to Abby for fifty years.

"We were," Abby reckons, "equal. At birth we weighed the same. . . . Although I was born sec-

ond, it was not as if I was a puny afterthought." Hardly.

ABIGAIL VAN BUREN

# The little boy from Brussels

was ironing-board skinny and plagued by headaches and colds. His immune system, he'd say later, seemed oddly askew. So for years doctors puzzled over the fragile child, until the boy's father, a florist and accountant, finally whisked his son to a gym.

"And that's when my life began," grins Belgian karate king Jean-Claude Van Damme, the "Muscles from Brussels" film star kickboxing his way into the spotlight, once yearly, with movie thrillers like *Double Impact*.

Thanks to a steady diet of karate, ballet, and weight lifting as a child, "I was totally cured physically and mentally from being a sickly weak kid," says the bicep-bulging actor, who captured a karate middleweight championship and the Mr. Belgium bodybuilding title by age twenty.

At twenty-six, he pushed his way into Hollywood with the martial-arts hit *Bloodsport*, though Van Damme's ambition and discipline yielded less impressive results in his love life, he confesses.

Van Damme's first marriage, to Maria "Millie" Rodriguez of Venezuela in 1980, lost out to ambition: "It was my fault because I was too young and only dreaming of movies. After four years, I sacrificed that marriage for my love for

my career. It was a long trip, and I knew I had to do it alone."

But in 1985, still penniless and unknown, Van Damme was working as a limo driver in L.A. and fell for Newport Beach beauty Cynthia Derderian, a feisty Californian he quickly married. She divorced Van Damme less than a year later, claiming he had physically abused her. Tabloids reported he would threaten her with his deadly trademark "helicopter kicks,'" then slap her with an open hand.

"No. No. No. We broke up because her father wanted me to give up show business and go into business with him. He said I'd never make it with my French accent. I wasn't ready to give up."

But what of the temper? "I've got a temper if somebody touches my movie—if they want to destroy the baby I create. Then I go crazy. I've got passion, but if I had slapped Cindy she'd die. . . ."

Then why her animosity? "She's still madly in love with me," claims Van Damme, "so she tried to hurt me. Now she's regretting the divorce because she sees my face all over *Cosmo* and *Playgirl*."

Indeed, Van Damme is soaring and finally happy, living in a $2 million San Fernando Valley estate with a third wife, bodybuilder Gladys Portugues,

whom he married in 1986, and their two small children, Kristopher and Bianca.

"When Gladys met me, I was a bum, but she *believed* in my dream, and it's a happy marriage," though Van Damme is frequently portrayed in the tabloids as a philandering husband. "My other wives wanted to fight to possess me—and couldn't support my dream," he notes.

How has the dream changed him? "I became more mature, more clever, more patient, but I'm still a big kid. The day I lose my dream, my sensitivity, my career is gone."

# JEAN-CLAUDE VAN DAMME

# Three years ago, the dismal

ratings hardly touched her. And unlike her career-minded friends, she had little interest in breaking away from the pitifully low-rated and now-defunct CBS news show *West 57th Street*.

"I was," Meredith Vieira recalls, "going through a rough, depressed period," bad-luck years filled with grief as the ambitious journalist tried and failed to have a baby.

The story starts in June 1986, when the reporter with the signature waist-length auburn hair married free-lance writer-producer Richard Cohen. "I'd never wanted children in any more than an intellectual way. My career was always my first priority. But with Richard, I discovered a tremendous yearning to create a family."

The yearning became an obsession. Pregnant in November of that year, Vieira viewed her pregnancy as nothing more than routine. "As a career woman, I assumed that when I was ready to have a baby, bingo—I'd have one. But the fetus died six weeks after conception. It was a total shock. I cried a tremendous amount, didn't believe I would ever conceive again."

In 1987, Vieira faced two more miscarriages: "The second time it was very quick—happened after four weeks—the third time I lost the baby at eight weeks."

By that time she was numb. "I didn't cry quite so much because I had become hardened to it—not wanting to attach as much significance to this life because of the pain involved."

Although her physician assured her a successful pregnancy was possible, and her husband refused to give up, "I didn't want to attempt it again because pregnancy to me meant miscarriage—not having a baby. I was the most depressed I'd ever been."

Only "a belief in something greater than me," Vieira says, persuaded her to try a fourth time, which resulted in a successful pregnancy.

"As I came to the end of my term, I suddenly feared birth defects. I thought: 'Why should *I* have a healthy baby?'"

Her fears were worsened by the news that the newborn was positioned incorrectly in the womb.

"He was head-up—a footling breach, standing with one leg up and one down."

But Benjamin Edwin, nicknamed Yummy, was born healthy. "And my whole perspective on life has changed," says Vieira, who eventually was fired by *60 Minutes*

producer Don Hewitt for being unavailable too much of the time.

"Having lost three children before Ben, I realized how fragile life can be. But I learned to have hope at times when things look hopeless. Now, I realize that having a child is worth any amount of pain.

"I agreed to *60 Minutes* on a part-time basis, but losing it was no tragedy. It's *just* a job—not the end-all, not what makes me tick. Ben is what really matters to me."

Happily, Vieira has since been hired by *CBS Morning News*.

# In 1945, the wartime romance

between a black American G.I. named Herman Watts and a Hungarian beauty, Maria Gufmitf, turned into a perfunctory marriage that gradually fizzled once the couple moved from bomb-blitzed Europe to Philadelphia.

"When I was fourteen, my parents finally divorced—but it was hardly the worst thing that ever happened to me," shrugs piano superstar André Watts, a man who has faced challenges well beyond Chopin, Liszt, and Rachmaninoff. He was traumatized, he confides, by those who viewed the Watts's interracial marriage as taboo.

"I was a scared, frightened and timid kid—good at running and jumping," says Watts, who recalls slowly coming to understand the poison of racism. "An interracial marriage at that time was not exactly high on the acceptance list. If you're both black and white, you don't belong to either race . . . you're sorta nowhere."

He saw himself as a foreigner, ostracized at age eight. "Every week, I got on a bus holding my mother's hand to go downtown for my piano lessons at the Philadelphia Music Academy and remember being stared at with absolute hostility by adults on the bus. 'Here comes this little brown

kid with his white mother.' That was the worst."

But the best revenge was just around the corner. When André was nine, he made his debut with the Philadelphia Orchestra, performing a Haydn concerto, and by sixteen he was "totally consumed by the piano."

Conductor Leonard Bernstein was captivated by his talent. "I flipped," Bernstein said at the time, predicting, "he'll walk in the footsteps of giants."

Bernstein chose Watts to substitute for an ailing Glenn Gould on January 31, 1963. "That was the first turning point in my life," says Watts, who performed the Liszt E-Flat Concerto to a thunderous ovation. The news of the virtuosic wunderkind was carried around the world. Watts was an instant star.

With no time to grow up emotionally, Watts threw himself into concerts, chaperoned by his mother until he was twenty-three.

"That was the next turning point," he says, "the year I got hepatitis from shellfish and was hospitalized." He had been unsure whether he really wanted to go through with some upcoming dates. "The doctor said I couldn't play for six months and I thought:

'Gee, isn't that great! Nobody can blame me for malingering here.'"

Why the ambivalence? "On some level, it was never my decision to become a concert pianist," he explains. "It was my mother's, Leonard Bernstein's, and circumstance," he says.

"I started to wonder if it was too late to do something else. But after three weeks in the hospital, I started going nuts, and was shocked at the vehemence with which I wanted to get back out onto the stage."

Watts, now forty-five and churning out a hundred concerts yearly, has never looked back. "I had realized deep inside, with just three weeks off the stage, that the thing I wanted to do most in my life was play. It took a kind of test like that to make sure. With all my nervousness and fear and anxiety, I think the piano is the happiest place for me."

239

# ANDRÉ WATTS

# Raquel Welch is an exercise

maniac. "I am indeed," she declares, a fifty-two-year-old wonder who became a yoga master at thirty-five and started breathing down Jane Fonda's neck in 1984 with her own beauty and fitness video programs—her recent *Lose 10 Pounds in Three Weeks* was on the video bestseller list.

"It works on *anybody*," claims the red-haired actress, who still sports the same 120-pound, 37–22$^1$/$_2$–35$^1$/$_2$ figure that allows her to wear a bikini.

"Movie stars," she chides, "aren't aging at the same rate as the regular population, which means we know something about keeping body and soul together—and losing those ten pounds when we need to."

Losing weight, however, was the last thing Welch had on her mind a few years ago when she faced a medical crisis that nearly killed her.

"I was scared to death," she says, remembering the day she was rushed to a Los Angeles hospital for a massive transfusion after intense menstrual bleeding: "I had been hemorrhaging on and off for nearly two years," says Welch, "and knew I couldn't be going through menopause because I was still ovulating.

"After I collapsed on the set of a movie, rumors started that I had cancer of the uterus. At that point, I thought I *might* be going through menopause—and was petrified of undergoing a hysterectomy."

Refusing to consider that option, the actress consulted "a wonderful specialist in Sacramento," gynecologist Dwane Townsend, who performed experimental laser surgery on her.

Six weeks later, Welch was exercising again. "I was, at that time, only the thirteenth woman in the world to have the operation," she says proudly. "Thank God I was able to avoid the dreaded hysterectomy. I hated the idea of my womb being taken out—an operation that I consider an unnecessary amputation—one that leaves a woman on hormones for the rest of her life.

"Women," she says, "are on the horizon of being able to avoid that kind of drastic surgery when they approach menopause, and I'm grateful I was able to avoid it right now."

Now back to her regular forty-five minute-per-day exercise routine, Raquel says she benefits from listening to her very own *Body & Mind*, a relaxation and stress-relief tape from HBO that addresses "not how you look on the outside, but how you feel inside. Thank God," she says, "I'm feeling good inside and out!"

# RAQUEL WELCH

# Behind the shutters of the

four-story red-brick row house on Frankfurt's Brahmsstrasse, scandal was afoot in the Orthodox Jewish household of Frau Siegel in 1928. Imagine, gossiped the neighbors, Selma Siegel's only son, Julius, impregnating the family's not-so-pretty new maid, Irma Hanauer, an uneducated daughter of a Wiesenfeld cattle dealer!

"But abortion," jokes the inimitable Dr. Ruth Westheimer, then known as Karola Ruth Siegel, "was not an option—for which I *thank God*—since I was the result of what must have been—to my grandmother—a devastating affair," a family sore spot replaced by more serious problems as the horror of Hitler's Germany loomed.

"My grandmother wouldn't leave Germany," says Westheimer. In late 1938, a few days after the notorious Kristallnacht, when synagogues and Jewish-owned businesses were attacked and destroyed by Nazis, ten-year-old Karola was awakened by harsh knocks on the door.

"The Nazis had come for my father—I can still remember their black shiny boots." Westheimer shudders. "They were not brutal, just firm. Daddy was a slightly built man and I remember him smiling faintly and waving good-bye. That was the last time I ever saw him."

Six weeks later, the little girl joined a *"Kinder transport"* of one hundred German-Jewish children sent to Switzerland by their families "until the trouble blew over . . . six months at the most," Westheimer recalls.

"I desperately didn't want to leave," she says, tears filling her eyes, "though my mother said, 'We will see each other again.'"

"But," says Westheimer, "I never saw my family again. Daddy and my grandmother died of starvation and exposure at Litzmanstadt, a Jewish ghetto in Poland; my mother was listed as *verschollen*, missing in action. I assume she died in Auschwitz."

After six years in Switzerland, Karola, then sixteen, emigrated to Palestine, later to France, and finally, in 1956, to the United States, where she would eventually earn her doctorate in family counseling. By 1980, she was spearheading with humorous panache her unique program of sexual literacy.

Yet despite international fame, a happy marriage to Fred Westheimer after two failed unions, and the comfort of two children, Miriam and Joe, she lives with tragic memories.

When did Westheimer finally come to terms with her family's deaths? "Actually, *never*," she admits. "I've never been able to bury them [psychologically] because the reality is that without the finality of a ceremony, you never have the feeling it's over."

The restless educator therefore cherishes new beginnings, such as her three soon-to-be-published books "and my new, my only grandson," she beams. "You've never seen a more gorgeous baby! When I look at my grandson I feel a *trrrremendous* satisfaction that Hitler was wrong—that he did not succeed in exterminating the Jews of the world."

# Dr. Ruth Westheimer

# She was a pregnant basketball

nut from Kokomo, Indiana, craving a baby boy and envisioning herself rooting for him on the sidelines. Then, three days after Jeanne White delivered her first-born, in December 1971, he was circumcised. "He bled for three days straight," recalls the unsuspecting mother, in the first of many medical tragedies she would face in her son's short life.

"Ryan was a severe hemophiliac—had less than one percent clotting agent in his blood. . . . Ryan got it from me. I blamed myself." But White's guilt and anger would be soothed by a son endowed with astonishing patience and sweet spirits. Years of painful hemorrhages in his joints required dozens of hospital stays. "Ryan always said he led a 'pretty normal life,' which always tickled me. *How* could anybody say this was normal? He saw kids next to him who were burn victims, who had cancer, or who were retarded."

And so, until Ryan White's thirteenth birthday, his hemophilia was controlled with a product called Factor VIII. "We thought it was a miracle drug, at $350 a shot. I injected the IV myself," says White. "Ryan could play Little League, he looked great, and we thought we were on easy street."

Then came December 17, 1984, and surgery. "After two hours," White recalls, "the doctor came out and told me Ryan had full-blown AIDS. I felt tremendous guilt. Imagine, unknowingly infecting my own son thousands of times!"

Given six months to live, the courageous boy shunned pity and attempted to return to school, but he was barred by local school officials. Eventually, after nine months of court battles, he won the right to attend school. "But," he writes in his posthumously published autobiography, *Ryan White: My Own Story*, "the prejudice was still there." Classmates tortured the boy with hateful epithets, angry parents blocked the school entrance, and one citizen shot through the front window.

The Whites were outlaws. "I couldn't believe the strength of their hate," fumes Jeanne White. "We lost *every* friend we had.

But newfound friends surfaced, like Michael Jackson, Elton John, and Elizabeth Taylor. And suddenly, Ryan White became a celebrity spokesman, "ripping the shame off the disease." "He taught people that you don't have to be gay or an IV drug user to get AIDS—that this disease affects everybody and must be stopped. He

wanted to be the only survivor, wanted to live long enough for a cure."

But in April 1990, even Ryan's hope began to fail him, his mother says. "'Mom, I'm really scared this time,' he told me. 'I'm getting tired of fighting this.' I knew he wasn't going to make it this time. I told him: 'Just let go, Ryan. It's all right, sweetheart.'

"But," she adds, tears filling her eyes, "I felt he was holding on because of me. It was very hard, because you never want to give up. Losing a child can never leave you. . . . The hurt is always there. I miss him, Oh God . . . ."

Now Jeanne White carries on the message of her son, publicizing the national AIDS hotline (1-800-342-AIDS) and raising money to fight the disease. "I guess it took a child to humanize AIDS," says White.

"Even when you think nothing worse can happen in life, it can happen. But you keep going. You can't wallow in self-pity."

# JEANNE WHITE

# At the 1911 coronation in

London, a Ruritanian prince picks up a chorus girl and they come to understand and respect each other. That's the plot of *The Prince and the Showgirl*, the 1957 film starring Marilyn Monroe and Laurence Olivier.

Now, for the modern-day version, how about "The Pop Singer and the Porn Star"? It would be a romance starring Margaret Whiting, who has recorded more than five hundred songs, and Jack Wrangler, twenty-seven years her junior, who starred in more than ninety pornographic films.

Talk about the Odd Couple. Before their accidental meeting in 1977 at a Broadway eatery, what emotional condition were they in? "Well," Whiting recalls, "I'd been unhappily married three times to men with big careers and egos and had learned to be careful about marriage. Before Jack, I felt happy, free, and had plenty of guys."

"I was doing a one-man show about the X-rated film industry," says Wrangler, another step in his fluke career that followed a stint at Northwestern University and attempts to make it as a legit actor.

Instead, he appeared in gay and straight films: "I was very eclectic. I could do *anything*, but in my personal life I was almost asexu-

al—a loner confused about what my future was going to be."

Then, somehow, on a hot summer night, both souls met. Magic? "I guess there must have been," says Wrangler. "One booth across from me was a lady with all this blond hair, a robust laugh, and lots of fur. I said, 'I gotta meet her, she looks like so much fun.'"

Whiting: "I was physically attracted, and thought he was very funny. When I went to see one of his adult films, it was very classic, like a ballet."

"I was also physically attracted to Margaret, but very confused," Wrangler recalls.

"The turning point in his life," says Whiting, "was when I said: 'Look, the adult films are very foolish for you. You're slamming a lot of doors. Leave at the top, get the hell out of it, walk away.'"

And so he has. Fourteen years after their meeting, Whiting, now a hearty sixty-eight, and a gray-haired Wrangler, forty-one, thrive. "Jack manages, directs, and writes the scripts for my cabaret act, and we're business partners," says Whiting, whose most recent album is *Then & Now*. Wrangler has written a musical, *Valentine*, is coauthoring a novel called *Sellout*, and is finishing the music and lyrics for

another musical based on the life of Johnny Mercer.

"Margaret," says Wrangler, "helped me to believe in myself as an artist and as a man—not a sex object. I might have wound up very depressed, jumping out of a window, but she gave me a second life."

Whiting: "We're not Hume Cronyn and Jessica Tandy, but we have a wonderful physical and mental relationship. Find love wherever you can!"

# Gene Wilder, who says he had

his "head up in the clouds" from the time he was eleven until he married the late Gilda Radner in 1984, is floating with the clouds once more. He's married again.

"When I was preparing for *See No Evil, Hear No Evil*," Wilder explains, referring to his 1989 movie with Richard Pryor in which Wilder played a timid deaf man, "I went to the New York League for the Hard of Hearing, and Karin Webb—an expert in helping people read lips—was assigned to help me prepare for the role." Love slowly blossomed.

But Wilder still has much to say about his late wife, to whom his marriage broke what he called a "fantasy state." Before that," says the actor, "I was dreaming about other lives, romantic situations, and falling in love.

"But Gilda was ringing a cowbell when we met . . . GONG, BONG GONG, GONG GONG. The message was: 'Get your head out of the clouds, come back to reality—*to real life with me*." Their happy marriage ended tragically when Radner died in 1989 after a two-and-a-half-year battle with ovarian cancer.

"Although those years were as close to hell as anything I'd known, now that I can breathe again I think it was the single greatest experience of my life," declares Wilder.

"It's hard to know about life until you are close to death. To see Gilda suffering on a daily basis—to watch her struggle . . . gave me another message about reality: 'Live in the moment.' What's important is *this hour*."

Getting over his anger took time. "After Gilda died," Wilder continues, "I would talk to her, scream, yell, cry without denying *any* of my feelings, so that there would be no ghosts haunting me for years to come. I felt I knew a terrible secret."

The secret? "Gilda didn't have to die. She was misdiagnosed. Her doctors were ignorant, believed her stomach pains were psychosomatic, meanwhile ignoring genetics—that her mother, grandmother, and cousin all died of ovarian cancer."

And, he says, they didn't give her a fifty-dollar blood test that could easily have detected Radner's cancer before it was too late.

Wilder has established the Gilda Radner Ovarian Detection Center at Cedars-Sinai Medical Center in L.A. (Call 1-800-OVAR-IAN), and recently inaugurated Manhattan's "Gilda's Active Patient Club." "If you're told you have cancer, you can come to this place with your children or mate to let out your furies and lighten the load," he says.

Any guilt about marrying again? "Nothing to feel guilty about. We fell in love very slowly. And remember Gilda had one message in life: *Live. Don't let anything kill your spirit*. I knew I had to be vulnerable again, or else I'd be killing the very thing she cherished."

# GENE WILDER

# The poor girl from Detroit's

Brewster Projects had wrapped herself in sequined gowns and traveled the world, thanks to a phenomenon called The Supremes.

Then, in 1970, disaster struck for Mary Wilson.

That was the year Diana Ross dumped the group—backup singer Mary and Flo Ballard—for a solo career. Mary faced seven years of hell, "marrying a monster," she says, and watching the revamped Supremes finally disintegrate in 1977.

"During those years I was fighting *the battle*," says the songstress, who told it all in *Supreme Faith*—a riveting autobiography that chronicled Wilson's dog days after Ross jumped ship.

"I was trying so hard to make the Supremes work," Wilson whispers, "make them strong without Diana."

Wilson hoped she would meet the right mate.

"What I thought I *needed*," she muses, "was a charismatic man who could handle any problem." That man turned out to be Santo Domingo-born Pedro Ferrer, whom she married in 1974.

"He was a handsome devil with a gorgeous Afro—dashing, charming, and seductive. Big deal!

"At first he gave me confidence, made me see that I had

so much to offer without Diane. But I also found out Pedro had a violent temper."

Exploding into jealous rages, Ferrer, Wilson remembers, "humiliated me in front of our three children by calling me a whore. He beat my face, gave me black eyes." He also punished the singer with violent sexual aggression.

"He used sex as a way of controlling and degrading me. I started the drinking and cocaine to deaden the pain, fearing that if I left him, I'd lose my children. His power over me was complete"—until the day in 1979 that Ferrer went too far.

"He beat my face to a pulp—the kids say I looked like *The Incredible Hulk*."

He slashed her face with a glass, nearly severing her ear. "That was it! I gave Pedro one year to clean up his act; he didn't and I walked."

The divorce became final in 1981. Since then, Wilson—now a single mother raising Pedro, Raphael, and Turquesa—has thrived in nightclubs, becoming financially secure, while also reclaiming her self-esteem.

"We women have to stand up and get control of our own lives rather than giving it away to abusive husbands. My heart breaks for

women who are totally alone in an abusive marriage. You cannot emerge from that hell unless you have some hope."

Wilson recommends hotlines like the National Coalition Against Domestic Violence, a twenty-four-hour toll-free hotline: 1-800-333-SAFE, "or therapy or a good lawyer. I've written my book to help women get over feeling frightened and ashamed to do all that."

# MARY WILSON

# She was born and bred a

Broadway Baby. Her stage mama, Nina, a Broadway wardrobe mistress, and dad, "Skip" Schipani, well-known Broadway concertmaster, pushed little Pia onto the stage right alongside Tallulah Bankhead in *Midgie Purvis* at age six, then swelled with pride when Pia at age eight tackled Broadway once again in *Fiddler on the Roof*. Not bad.

By age seventeen, having equated her self-esteem "totally on getting good parts and avoiding negative reviews—pretty sad," the Polish girl from Brooklyn was a hard-boiled Broadway soubrette.

"Everybody thought I was the toughest thing in town—don't tangle with me," laughs Pia Zadora. "Yet I was desperately insecure, had never been allowed to be a kid, and couldn't trust anybody my own age. That's why I needed somebody a lot more secure, a lot more nurturing," somebody like Meshulam Riklis, an Israeli immigrant who has created a business empire worth $620 million today.

"Rik chased and chased me until I finally caught him," giggles Pia, remembering the night in 1972 she met the man who would provide her the emotional security she craved.

"Rik was then forty-eight, me seventeen. There I was in Columbus, Ohio, starring in a road production of *Applause*, and Rik was in town lecturing, dragged to the show by my manager. He had lost and owed millions at the time— was almost bankrupt—but who cared? He brought me a flower backstage and asked me out to dinner. I was a very proper Catholic virgin and brought along to dinner my big rag doll, Rina. Rik liked Rina," Pia says, though he lost interest in Pia after six dates.

"Yeah, he thought I was a pain in the neck, which *intrigued* me. That was a challenge. In New York," goes Pia's version, "he was known as the sheikh of Fifth Avenue, the King of the Jews, and had lots of *Cosmo* cover girls banging on his door. But he wanted *me*! The first year he had to win over my mother; the second and third years, he was working his way back financially; the fourth year we argued over wedding invitations. And when his parents heard their Jewish son was marrying a *shiksa*, they moved away to Israel! *Everybody* was saying: 'It's an old man and a young girl and it's going to last five minutes!'"

Instead, the marriage has lasted fifteen years and produced two children, Kadie and Christopher. "I would say Rik is part father figure, best friend, and lover. He's helped me to believe in myself. Also, beyond show business, I've learned from Rik that there has to be some *anchor* in life— to me it's the family."

How has the twenty-nine-year difference in ages affected Pia and Ricklis? "Now I feel old and he feels young. On his sixtieth birthday, I sent him a card saying: 'Age is a matter of the mind; if you don't mind, it doesn't matter!'"

253

# Epilogue

He was a miserably unhappy child—paper-clip skinny, unathletic, and constantly taunted. Nobody protected him. And the coward, terrified of fighting back himself, stared out the window at school each day, floating in fantasy, mindlessly twisting his hair and dreading the hour of gym class.

On his tenth birthday, he and his mother were pulled into the principal's office in Eggertsville, New York, to discuss the ramifications of a D– average.

"Don't feel bad," Principal Northrup told the mother. "Although your son has a low IQ, garbage collectors can be happy, too."

To escape the humiliation of bad grades, the boy began piano lessons and turned an above-average affinity into a cottage industry. By thirteen, the kid nicknamed "Fingers" was banging out Chopin nocturnes and his own ragtime version of "Alley Cat." By eighteen he had escaped into pianoland altogether, burying himself for the next nine years at a conservatory of music.

Imprisoned in the isolation of a practice room, the young man was now dreaming of a concert career, though never quite believing it possible. Somehow he was unable to shed a painful self-consciousness—his hands and legs trembled during recitals.

Finally, at age twenty-six, suffering from ulcerative colitis, barely able to play with the tendons of his arms locked in spasms, and never having had a job or earned a dime, he quit the piano, borrowed three hundred dollars and moved from Baltimore to New York.

Unconsciously, with desperation his guide, he plucked from midair a solution, concocting the fantasy of writing the biography of his favorite pianist, Vladimir Horowitz, a task that took four years—years followed by more writing, high hopes, fingers typing, with self-esteem rising, slowly.

The words of the kid's seventh-grade English teacher, Mrs. Breverman, came echoing back in time: "He should write."

He does now, he's grateful, and he has learned that careers don't travel in straight lines, that turning points happen when they need to, that when one dream fails, another can take its place, even if a kid has a "low IQ."

That kid was me.

# GLENN PLASKIN